D1534840

THEORY OF AUDITING

Evaluation, Investigation, and Judgment

Publication of this book was made possible through a grant from
ARTHUR ANDERSEN & CO.

THEORY OF AUDITING

Evaluation, Investigation, and Judgment

Charles W. Schandl

SCHOLARS BOOK CO.
4431 Mt. Vernon
Houston, Texas 77006

Library of Congress Cataloging in Publication

Schandl, Charles W.
    Theory of auditing.

    Includes index.
    1. Auditing. I. Title.
HF5667.S28   657'.45   78-17862
ISBN O-914348-23-X

Manufactured in the United States of America

*Dedicated to the victims
of false judgments, poor audits, and wrong decisions*

CONTENTS

PREFACE

THIS BOOK was written in the years from 1969 to 1975. Events since 1969 have shown the need for a comprehensive theory of auditing, including the philosophical and psychological foundations. I have attempted to integrate into one system the findings of the semantic philosophy, the communication theory, and the psychology of thinking. I have tried to apply them to the evaluation process and the judgment. I adopted the broadest possible definition of auditing in order to explore the deepest foundations of audit activity, the communication process, and human thinking as they apply to problem-solving and judgment.

Parts of the book were presented to the American Accounting Association, Canadian Regional meeting, in June, 1971 (Montreal, Province of Quebec) and in June, 1974 (Toronto, Ontario). The first paper contained the discussions of the Definition of Auditing and the Structure of the Audit and the listing of some of the Principles. I submitted the paper for presentation at the AAA Conference in Lexington, Kentucky, in 1970. The paper was not included in the program because the Progress Report of the AAA Committee on Basic Auditing Concepts occupied the part of the program available for auditing. But as the paper was in the possession of at least two members of the AAA Committee, I have reason to believe that it had an influence on the content and findings of the Final Report (the ASOBAC).[1]

In 1969 I failed to recognize the place of the purpose (goals) in the structure (system) of the evaluation process, and I was not yet able to find the place of the audit in the decision-making process. I am indebted to the AAA Report on Accounting Theory Construction and Verification for leading me to the differentiation between the attention-directing, verification, and decision audits.[2]

---

[1] "Report of the Committee on Basic Auditing Concepts," *Accounting Review*, Supplement (Sarasota, Fla., 1972).

[2] "Accounting Theory, Construction and Verification" (The T. H. Williams Report), *Accounting Review*, Supplement (Sarasota, Fla., 1971).

I quote from Mautz and Sharaf:

> The remainder of this volume is concerned with the
> development of a small number of what we conceive
> to be the primary concepts of auditing. These are:
> evidence, due audit care, fair presentation, indepen-
> dence, and ethical conduct. We do not claim complete-
> ness for this list. There may well be other significant
> concepts which should be added. On the other hand,
> we are confident that each of these occupies an important
> position in the structure of auditing theory. We hope
> that others will be moved to add to this type of analysis
> until in time all the useful concepts of this discipline
> have been stated and subjected to philosophical exami-
> nation.[3]

I attempted to take up their challenge and, starting with the
fundamentals, I took the evaluation process, the judgment, the
investigation, and evidence under a magnifying glass in order
to establish and analyze concepts, their relationship, and their
proper use. In my attempt, I am certainly stretching the patience
of the reader. But I hope that he will gain an insight into the
most important area of human activities and that he will become
a wiser and, therefore, a better person.

Galileo Galilei met with hostile reception when he presented
his telescope to his fellow scientists. His colleagues refused to
look into the telescope. Those who finally agreed to look into
it accused him of fraud, alleging that he put painted pictures
in the tube.

To read the present book requires more effort than looking
into a telescope. My magnifying glass wandered around deeper
and in a bigger field than just a part of the surrounding landscape.
At least, I shall not be accused of fraud! Perhaps when my former
students become auditors, lawyers, managers, and judges, they
will fulfill their tasks better.

Finally, I would like to thank Mrs. Mary Shook, B.S., M.S.,
(Connecticut) for her altruistic help in producing a readable copy

---

[3] R. K. Mautz and Hussein A. Sharaf, *The Philosophy of Auditing* (Madison, Wis.:
American Accounting Association, 1961), p. 67.

of my manuscript; Mrs. J. C. Casey for producing a printable copy of my manuscript; Professors Thomas J. Burns (Ohio State University) and Kenneth F. Byrd (McGill University) for reading my manuscript and encouraging me in my work; and Arthur Andersen & Co. for the grant which made possible the publication of this book.

INTRODUCTION

THE AREAS OF human knowledge are increasing every day. New knowledge acquired by the extension of our sensory organs, new organization of the acquired knowledge in new areas, and new theories are permanent features of our century.

Yet, auditing, as a field of activity centered around the professional accountant, the internal auditor, and the operational auditor, seems to be caught in a frustrating and stationary situation. We have textbooks on the audit procedures recommended for public accountants in their statutory audit, a few articles on auditors' legal responsibilities, and an enquiry into the philosophy of auditing by R. K. Mautz and Hussein A. Sharaf, published in 1961.[1] In no other discipline can we find less literature in the last 150 years than in the field of auditing.

Auditing was "done" but was never analyzed as a scientific activity. The "art of auditing" was supposed to be acquired by imitation, by doing what an expert did, by imitating the auditors in the field. And there was no theory of auditing; there was not even a proper definition of auditing. Yet, definition is the cornerstone, the foundation for the study of every discipline and its theory.

Once the proper definition is established, then the body of knowledge is determined; and the theory, with its postulates, structure, principles, and standards, can be established simply by following the usual methods of philosophical analysis.

The area of a discipline consists of actual phenomena (practice, facts) and the underlying theory. The theory is a system of ideas or statements held as an explanation or account of a group of facts or phenomena and is based on the acceptance of a structure. It could also be considered as a statement of the general rules and principles or the causes of the facts observed in the area of a discipline.

---

[1] R. K. Mautz and Hussein A. Sharaf, *The Philosophy of Auditing* (Madison, Wis.: American Accounting Association, 1961).

The theory itself consists of:

1. Postulates, theorems
2. Structure (model)
3. Principles
4. Standards

These elements, together with the actual practice, compose the whole area of a certain discipline.

Postulates are propositions that are demanded or claimed to be granted. They are fundamental concepts, or assumptions, that are required to be accepted without proof.

Theorems are propositions that can be explained by postulates. They are similar to postulates, as they have to be accepted as propositions, but their validity is based on more fundamental postulates. They are convenient resting points in an inquiry for basic postulates.

Structure explains the parts and their interrelationship in a discipline (model of concepts).

Principles are conventions that are commonly associated with a discipline, serving as explanations for practices. They are norms that can be followed or not.

Standards are required quality of procedures in a certain discipline. They originate in the community under different social forces; they may or may not be formulated by the governing body, the state.

WHY THEORY?

Theory is necessary because it is useful, when usefulness can be discussed from the point of view of an individual and of a group. "A number of isolated facts does not produce a science any more than a lump of bricks produces a house. The isolated facts must be put in order and brought into mutual structural relations in the form of some theory. Then, only, do we have a science, something to start from, and analyze, ponder on, criticize and improve."[2]

[2] A. Korzybski, *Science and Sanity*, 4th ed. (Lakeville, Conn.: The International Non-Aristotelian Library Publishing Co., 1958), p. 55.

An individual uses theory for several purposes. The first purpose of theory is to help in the understanding of the facts in a discipline. The theory explains the phenomena; it reduces them to components. The individual uses the theory in order to organize the data provided by outside stimuli into information. The theory is a help in the storage and recall of information. Without it we can be overpowered by the multitude of data originating in the outside world. The theory, the proper and organized classification of information, allows immediate and proper recall when judgment and action are needed in a problem situation. It is an always available tool, ready for application in any situation. The theory facilitates the communication between individuals. It is a preset system to reduce the use of signs and words and their interpretations.

Theory has an impact on the future behavior of the people who adhere to it and also on the opinions and behavior of the people who reject it. Theory facilitates learning, remembering, and teaching. The instruction of facts without establishing the theory in the minds of the students is not effective. The fact will fade in the learner's mind much faster without theoretical ties and organization than with their support.

Theory has a profound influence on the attitudes of a group or society that accepts it and adheres to it. The theory can create blind spots in the interpretation and understanding of data. But it also creates interest, inquiry, and research into areas that have not been fully explained or are improperly organized within its framework.

The theory creates a system of values, norms for an individual or society, determining their judgments about phenomena, problems, and standards in a certain field.

We find no "theory" in the natural world around us. If a Martian from outer space should appear and say to me, "Show me a piece of theory," I could not show it. Theory is the result of our cognitive processes and the result of generalizations and abstractions. It exists in us; it can be considered as an imaginary system that can be discovered by making inferences from writings, words, or actions of individuals. It may be laid down in writing, in a more or less systematic form; or it may be adapted, used by an individual who is not even aware of it.

The awareness and knowledge of the theories underlying our actions allow us to perform our actions better and more efficiently.

DEVELOPMENT OF A THEORY

How do we develop a theory that is usable for predicting the future events or a quality of some future event?

Evidently the first task is to delineate, to define the areas of the past and present, and to determine the field to be explored.

The next step is to analyze the events—the activities—in the area by breaking them down into interrelated parts. Then we have to observe the relationship of the parts in action, in time. We can arrive at a series of interrelationships, connections, and functions. Theory is, in effect, nothing else but the system of relationships of certain concepts that are assumed to be the fundamental concepts of the discipline.

We have to put in the center the activities of the human individual or group, perhaps both.

Once we have arrived at a detailed model of the activities, the postulates will be easy to find. From the model and the postulates, the principles to be followed in an activity present themselves almost automatically.

In this book I will attempt to follow the method outlined above. Because the total picture will appear only at the end of our investigation, I ask that the reader be patient.

CHAPTER 1

THE DEFINITION AND THE POSTULATES

IN THE LITERATURE we find several descriptions and explanations of the terms "audit" and "auditing":

1. Examination of documents before their recording or settlement (voucher audit).
2. Appraisal or investigation to determine adherence to prescribed procedures (internal audit, procedural audit).
3. Inspection of records by persons other than the personnel who keep them (income tax audit, workmen's compensation).
4. An objective examination of financial statements initially prepared by management (audit by a public accountant). [1]
5. Investigation and appraisal of operations by persons outside the ordinary line organization (operational audit).
6. Appraisal of effectiveness of management by outsiders (management audit). [2]

The above definitions of auditing are not "definitions" in the logical meaning of the concept. They describe the various applications of the audit concept in different, usually business oriented, areas. They arose from the practical need to give the students and professionals a definition which is satisfactory in the pursuit of further study in the relatively narrow area of a special application of the audit activity. They are not satisfactory as a foundation for an attempt to construct a theory of auditing, as they do not

[1] H. F. Stettler, *Auditing Principles* (Englewood Cliffs, N. J.: Prentice-Hall, Inc., 1960); similar: J. W. Cook and G. M. Winkle, *Auditing: Philosophy and Technique* (Boston: Houghton Mifflin Co., 1976).
[2] E. L. Kohler, *A Dictionary for Accountants*, 3rd ed. (Englewood Cliffs, N. J.: Prentice-Hall, Inc., 1963), s.v. "audit."

allow for the broader and general aspects of the audit concept.

A logical and correct definition is based on the structure of categories or concepts. The definition has to indicate the broader, or more general, category, as well as the "differentia specifica" (specific differences) that differentiate the concept to be determined from the other concepts in the same general field.

The philosophical or logical definition of auditing has to be general enough to encompass the six fields indicated above, yet narrow enough to differentiate auditing from other fields where our findings could not be considered valid.

The broadest concept we can find in the six definitions is that of a *human activity*. No doubt, auditing is a "human activity," subject to all inferences due to the human nature. Our knowledge of the activities of nonhuman (animal) behavior is too limited to allow any information about nonhuman beings performing similar activities, so we have the right to disregard in our inquiry their similar functions. There is no doubt that auditing is an activity, as it requires a series of mental and sometimes physical steps in the performance of the process. The category of "human activities" is an extremely broad one. We have to look now for the specific features identifying the audit activity within this large field.

A common feature of all descriptions of the audit activity mentioned above is that they are *evaluation* processes. Evaluation is a comparison, resulting in an opinion or judgment. As a comparison, it implies the existence of a state of affairs (a model) and the existence of another (actual, possible, or imaginary) state of affairs. In the process of evaluation we consider both situations and, from viewing them concurrently in our mind, we arrive at one of several conclusions.

The number of states of affairs (or models) to be evaluated or considered can be more than two, and their structure is usually not finalized in our imagination. We can develop the different models as we proceed with our evaluation, obtain new data, and develop new information.

We may consider the evaluation process as consisting of five, sometimes six, distinct mental steps or phases:

1. A purpose, a goal, for the evaluation process. The purpose

will determine all the following parts of the whole process.

2. The establishment or acceptance of a group or system of norms (criteria).
3. The determination of the state of affairs or states of affairs to be evaluated by accepting data or by collecting evidence.
4. The actual comparison, a mental activity consisting of the viewing of possible causes and possible effects of the divergencies or convergencies between the normative and the other, actual or planned, system of established group of facts or events.
5. The opinion, or judgment. In the opinion or judgment phase of evaluation, we relate our findings, our groups of comparisons, to the purpose, or goal, of our evaluation. We establish the relevance of the convergencies or divergencies, the materiality, and we arrive at an opinion.
6. If the evaluation is not for our own purposes but for the purposes of another individual or group, we have to report our findings to the other party or parties. In this case, a sixth step is necessary in our evaluation procedure—the *reporting* of our conclusions and findings, depending on the desired extent of the information.

At this stage of our search for the definition of auditing, we arrive at it as *a human evaluation process.*

This definition would encompass such activities as selections between alternatives—decision-making in the broadest sense of the word—and is evidently too loose and too general. We go to a store to buy shoes. We have our set of norms: the shoes have to fit us, to be within a certain price range, and to be of a certain color. The selection of the shoes that we buy is a process of evaluation; it is decision-making, but evidently we cannot call it auditing. So we have to narrow the concept by introducing the purpose of the evaluation (the "why") process.

In audits of type 1 (voucher audit), the purpose of the evaluation is the establishment of the validity or the reliability of the data contained in the documents before their recording or settlement. The same is the purpose of the evaluation process in the case of audits of types 3 and 4 (inspection of records by outsiders, and public accountants' audit of the financial statements). We receive some data, as, for example, financial statements or income tax returns, and we have to establish the validity or reliability of those data.

In audits of type 2 (internal audit), type 3 (operational audit), and type 4 (management audit), the purpose of the evaluation process is the establishment of adherence to certain norms. Those norms might be the procedures or policies prescribed by management, or they might be the norms of efficiency of operations or sound management; but the validity of data, or truth, is also a norm. So we may use the "establishment of adherence to certain norms" instead of "establishment of validity of data" as a broader concept for our definition of auditing.

Finally, we arrive at a definition of auditing, which follows:

> AUDITING IS A HUMAN EVALUATION PROCESS TO ESTABLISH
> THE ADHERENCE TO CERTAIN NORMS, RESULTING IN AN OPINION
> (OR JUDGMENT).

Is the new definition of auditing too broad?

Certainly it expands the concept of auditing to include activities until now not considered to be auditing.

The evaluation process to establish adherence to certain norms is widely used in almost every aspect of human life. According to this definition, if I check my children's clothing in the morning before they leave for school, I audit.

If I proofread a letter typed by our secretary, I audit.

Somebody tells me what happened at a meeting. Before accepting the report as a fact, I compare it to my previous experiences and my previous information, and I audit the new information.

The judge in court proceedings hears data, perhaps conflicting with those of others, and evaluates them as to their validity before establishing a model of what actually happened. He audits the pieces of evidence presented. Then he compares the system of accepted facts—an organized picture of past events—to the legal norms that he has to apply; he audits again. So in developing a judgment, the judge has to go through two distinct audit activities.

In the interdisciplinary activity called operations research, we also find two different phases of audit activities: First is the evaluation of the validity of primary source data. It is futile to analyze situations without knowing which of the data are reliable, which are probably reliable, and which are not reliable. Later the result (the model of planned operations) has to be tested as to efficiency, practicability, and so forth. This testing is the second audit step in operations research.

In the field of physical sciences, we audit information whenever we test somebody else's findings or generalizations (laws).

We can generalize from the above exemplification that the audit is a necessary component in every information whenever we evaluate the validity of the information.

In information or communication studies, we distinguish between raw data—or source information—and information. The raw data are impulses that a receiver gets from outside sources or from his (its) own memory, and the information is the resulting effect, idea, or knowledge that is developed by the receiver. The audit function has a place in the information or communication field at two levels again: first, the evaluation of the validity of raw data; second, the evaluation of the validity of resulting information.

The audit function is therefore an important part of the communication process. It follows that we have to consider the audit and the theory of auditing as integral parts of the developing science of communication. The findings of communication science and theory at the scientific level have to be valid for auditing. On the other hand, the practical wisdom that has been accumulated through centuries by the auditing profession has validity and value for the communication science and theory.

When speaking about communication science, I use the qualifying expression "at the scientific level." Communication science and information theory are relatively new fields of knowledge. And as is every literature in a new field, the literature about information and communication is full of valueless publications, verbalizations, and simple truisms which are hidden behind the façade of freshly invented pseudoscientific terminology which has been watered down to fill a study or a book. Only in 1968 and 1969 did I come across books deserving to be called "scientific" publications on information or communication theory.

Because auditing is as much a part of the communication science as evaluation of data and information, we have to outline a few basic features of communication and information theory and perhaps enrich our knowledge in the fields of communication by introducing some new concepts or structures. (For a thorough study of the field up to 1968, I have to refer to Professor Lee Thayer's excellent book, *Communication and Communication Systems.*[3]) Almost every study of communications starts with the simple and basic assumption: A (the emitter, or source) communicates data to B (the receiver), and X (the information) results. It is evident that the basic model in this abstract form is a model of communication that is valid only in the field of nonliving receivers (machinery).[4]

If we consider B a living person, we have to broaden the basic model as follows:

A (source) communicates data (message) to B (the receiver). B (the receiver) is exposed concurrently to the data (messages) from various other sources and to data provided by his memory (storage), and X (the information) results. This is sketched in Figure 1.

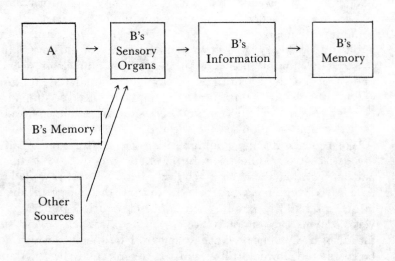

Figure 1

[3] Lee Thayer, *Communication and Communication Systems in Organization, Management, and Interpersonal Relations* (Homewood, Ill.: R. D. Irwin, 1968).
[4] *Ibid.*

In the field of mechanical communications we try to eliminate the data from other sources (called noise or interference). In communications where the receiver is a person, we cannot control all of his sensory organs, and, therefore, we cannot eliminate them. It remains the function of B to evaluate the validity of messages (audit of data) and to evaluate the validity of resulting information (audit of information).

If we are interested in the validity, usefulness, or reality of information, we have to introduce the audit function, as we have to evaluate data and information in the light of some norms. Those norms or criteria may be validity, reality, relevance, desirability, and so on.

THE PYRAMID OF DATA

A concept, which at the moment is new to the field of communication theory, is the "Pyramid of Data" or the "Pyramid of Surrogates."

The data sources, or memories of information, are usually thought of as an unorganized mass of events, judgments, pictures, and so forth. In some cases, a part of the total memory may be regarded as more or less organized within a conceptual framework. Mechanical memories are organized as filing systems for data that have been reduced to systems of symbols.

When we consider the relationship between the volume of data in a message emitted by a source and the total field of processed information or data available in the memory of the source, we have to realize that the information available for a message has to be considered as having a structural shape similar to that of a pyramid (if viewed in three dimensions) or a triangle (if viewed in two dimensions).

On the base of the pyramid we have all the detailed data that has been stored in the memory system, and as we proceed up in our pyramid, the data become more and more generalized. In the summarization (or generalization) process we lose details—we lose some parts of the information—and we maintain other details in a more generalized form. Finally, at the top of the pyramid, we have only one concept with one judgment left.

As an example, let us consider the system of accounting records and reports. From an infinite number of transactions, by determining the entity of accounting and the time period, we set up the proper organization to record data on the so-called source documents (invoices, vouchers, etc.). The total of the source documents is the base of our pyramid. In the journals, the source documents are classified and summarized. Some valuable information (e.g., the addresses of customers, the type of merchandise sold, etc.) is lost in the journalizing process. By summarizing the journals we make another step in our pyramid and again have restricted the volume of available sources of information (data) for purposes of emission.

The summarized totals of the journals are posted to the general ledger accounts, and again we have a reduction in the quantity of data in the general ledger. The next reduction results in the trial balances taken from the ledgers.

From the trial balances we arrive at the financial statements. And from there it is just another step to the net income figures or total equity figure, depending on which one we consider the most relevant or needed in a given situation.

Our pyramid can be considered as two-, three-, or multiheaded, if we consider two, three, or more data as needed for our data emission or information purposes.

The concept of the data or raw information pyramid is applicable to every type of data, not only to business data.

Imagine yourself taking the witness stand: You have to give testimony about something you have seen. You could tell the story with detailed description, going into details for hours or even days, proceeding as Honoré de Balzac did in his works. But you are limited to a few minutes, so you omit the incidentals. In effect, you realize that the data received and recorded by you in your visual memory could provide more data for the potential receivers, and you could speak for six hours, three hours, one hour, or only five minutes. You have in your mind a pyramid-like structure of raw source data. You anticipate that you have thirty minutes for your testimony, so the irrelevant (according to your judgment) data are omitted, and you try to convey the relevant or important data in the thirty minutes.

You could reduce the testimony to a short statement: "A man was killed." Evidently those words, conveying information from the top level of the pyramid, would be too general for the purposes of the judge and jury, and you anticipate this. You aim at the level of usability of the data by the receivers.

We cannot find the data pyramid in nature. We can construct a model of data storage, resembling the pyramid in every data-processing and -storing system. We accept the concept for the visualization of the data stored within ourselves and other human beings because it will be useful for our further inquiries into communication and information.

THE SLANTING OF THE PYRAMID

The data pyramid is a creation of our minds. It exists in our imaginations, like the concept of a number (for example, number seven). We cannot see in nature the number seven. We are familiar with a sign—7—and we identify it as a man-made concept, as a concept of measurement, but we cannot see it in the physical world surrounding us. We know from experience that the concept exists in the minds of our fellow human creatures.

We shall not conceptualize the data pyramid as a rigid one. From the same data base, we may construe an infinite number of pyramids, each of them slanted differently. Each pyramid's shape is determined by its peak.

We may be interested, not in the net profit figure derived from the multitude of data contained in documents recorded in an accounting data system, but in the quantity and type of merchandise sold in a territory. Our peak will be the data required. The pyramid containing the pertinent data will be different from the net profit pyramid.

In the case of the testimony about the event that we have seen, we may summarize the event by saying, "It was a rainy day." The data subordinated to this message have to be visualized as a pyramid having a different shape from the pyramid underlying the data "A man was killed." With other words, every simple statement (or data emitted) can be considered to be a peak of the data pyramid, and every extension of the simple statement has to be regarded as a broadening of the peak. We may go on, reaching deeper into our memory for more and more details, finally arriving at the bottom: the total of our memories or sources of information available.

We are unable to transfer all the data available in our memory or all the data existing in an artificial man-made memory. Therefore, we have to reduce the data in quantity in order to make them transferable. This basic phenomenon of communications is the fact, which is expressed in the concept of data pyramid.

To make the data transfer possible in a world limited by time, energy, and the receiver's capacity to absorb information, we have to reduce the infinite quantity of potential data to workable, transmittable, and absorbable quantities. We are doing it by omitting from the potential sources of information a multitude of details considered unimportant or irrelevant.

The receiver, or user, of information is expecting the data reduction in most of the communicative situations existing in the society. As receivers, we are preprogrammed to receive reduced data, depending on our relationship to the source of communication and our expected usage, if any, of the data received.

The judge does not expect that a witness shall take the stand for five days while telling what he has seen in an accident. A potential creditor of a business firm would be horrified if we presented to him all the sales invoices of the borrower for a given period.

We are forced by sheer limitations of time and energy to reduce the data to transmittable and intelligible size by the omission of irrelevant details and repetitions. The data reduction can be visualized as the transmittance of data from a lower level of the data pyramid; and depending on what is omitted, the shape and direction of the data pyramid is different. *The pyramid of data is slanted differently, depending on the direction of the data reduction process.* We may say that the pyramids are slanted depending on the anticipated relevance of the data for the user.

From a given mass of primary data sources—or, in the case of an individual, from a mass of primary perceptions—we may construct an infinite number of pyramids, each having a distinct peak and each having a different shape, depending on the needs set by the goal of the audit and the structure of the norm system to be used for the judgment.

The data pyramid is built on an area, the *principal* determined by the goal of the judgment, and it consists of *surrogates* at different levels of abstraction.[5]

THE USER OF DATA

It was perhaps unfortunate to discuss the data and the structure of the data before we discussed the receiver (or user) of the data. In our lopsided way of looking at things, we started with the data and the originator of the data, as is done in almost every book or article dealing with the subject, because chronologically (in time sequence) it comes first; but conceptually it is the receiver of the data which is first.

Without reception and understanding, the data are not data. They are fading signals of a reality that remains unknown. Unless I conceive something as data or perceive something as perception, the data as sources of information do not exist. We cannot see the bacteria unless we convert the data emitted by those bacteria into data that are perceivable by our eyes or other sensory organs. We receive data through our sensory organs. Data received will be stored in the memory of a living person or animal. We say that they are understood if they fit in the historically (by experience) developed system of concepts, ideas, judgments, and stereotypes of the individual. The individual will use the data stored and transformed into information within his memory as instruments in making decisions, in solving problems, and so forth. A living organism may act on data without the interjection of the memory, but then we are speaking about reflexes and not about conscious actions. The transforming, conceptualizing function of the memory, the perpetual change in the memory's content and structure, and the use of information derived in the memory from data and the unity of memory in time are the characteristic features of living creatures having a self-consciousness. We use the term "information" to describe the concepts and ideas that are created by the living memory from data received either in the past or recently. Mechanical or electro-mechanical information systems are not creating information. They are transmitting elements of data that can be regenerated, stored, and eventually transformed

[5] See also J. H. Wigmore, "Structure of Evidence," *Students' Textbook of the Law of Evidence* (Chicago, Ill.: Foundation Press, 1935), pp. 40–41.

into other data. Data become information in the living mind when they are understood.

The individual who is creating information from data is bombarded continuously by a multitude of data. The attention, the selection of data for reception, is a problem in itself, and we will probably see an expansion of the literature and research dealing with the problem of "getting the attention." The designers of mechanical or electronic data-processing equipment also have problems with "not required" or "hostile" data (noise) and data destruction. But the problems are small compared to the problem of human receivers of data. The data provided by our senses, by our hearing, reading, and so forth, are so many, so complex, and so uncontrollable that it is nonsense to create a term and write about "total information system," or "integrated information system." They are terms created by skillful advertising men in order to glorify their magnetic filing machine, the computer.

Figure 2 illustrates how the communication of data and creation of information may be modified to show more details and be closer to reality.

THE DECISION AND THE ACTION

The user, the central figure of the study of communication at our level, may act immediately on the receipt of the data without intervention of the memory. This action is called reflex or conditioned reflex. If the data are perceived through the memory and become information, an action may or may not follow.

What is the relationship of the action and the information?

During the past ten years we were flooded by literature trying to explain and even to teach decision-making and problem-solving. Models of decision-making and problem-solving were presented in literature of management. The models of decision-making created the image of manager as an abstract creature, weighing alternative methods of action and selecting relevant information.

We have to realize that this type of decision maker, who is logical, remote from the social surrounding, and impersonal, is only an abstraction; it is just as nonexistent as the "homo oeconomicus" of the classical economists of the 19th century. The abstract decision maker or problem solver is similar to a mannequin in

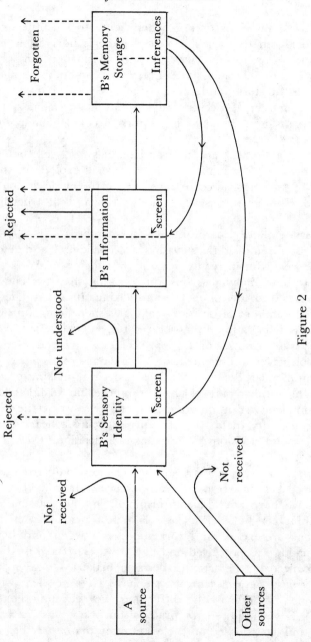

Figure 2

a store window. It is only a paper figure to illustrate or show the dresses on display. The fact that he is not real is hidden in the use of expressions like "relevant information," in assigning figures to unmeasurables like "uncertainty," and in the assumption that he is "ahistoric" and operating in a vacuum. I am not saying that this model of decision maker has no usefulness, but its usefulness is limited to the limited purposes of elementary instruction.

We see models of an atom and models of a cell, but we do not expect that the model of the atom shall explode or that the model of the cell shall come alive. And if the model is not useful any more for our purposes, we can discard it and construct another one.

We will explore decision models in Chapter 2.

It is usually implied that decision is a cool, logical, and determinable process. But in reality it is far from being so. We act more often without making a conscious decision than by following a deliberate and definite decision-making process. The overwhelming amount of decision-making is sheer imitation, without conscious deliberation. In most cases it is a mental reflex. Whether conscious or unconscious, (reflex) decisions are based on imaginations constructed of elements of our memory.

Naturally, it is easy to describe the decision-making process or the problem-solving process in one sentence, but we did not answer and cannot answer the questions: How do we construct the elements of our memory (data bank) in forms having a bearing on our behavior and decisions? And what is a decision? Does it result always in action?

In practice we can discover the decisions only from actions, perceived as such. We hardly can perceive a decision "not to act," unless we have additional information on the decision maker. One thing can be asserted, as it is almost a truism: Actions and decisions are based on information. But when and how this information was perceived and how it was corrected or distorted (reorganized by the actor or decision maker), we cannot know. Psychologists and psychoanalysts have tried to deal with the problems, but due to the difficulties they encountered, a new approach was required for practical purposes; this was *behavioralism,* and it was based on the assumption that *members of a group in a community will behave in the near future as they did in the immediate past.*

This approach, although not completely reliable, is accepted for practical purposes in the field of applied social sciences, such as business administration, law, and so forth, and it is the only one that is practically usable for the purposes of our investigation.

HOW DATA BECOME INFORMATION

How will data become information?

The world inside and outside of our skins is a largely complex, unending sequence of events. Some of those events of the world are within the limited range of our sensory equipment (with or without amplification or translation by some technological device). These particular events or occurrences are therefore *potential data* for us. As long as these events are within range (or in the physical form necessary to be registered by our sensory equipment), they will infringe upon that equipment as data available to us about some aspect of our internal or external environments. At this point, however, those events exist only as raw sensory data (having been translated from that prior state as physical sound waves, light waves, etc.).

The next step in this sequence is a selective conversion of this sensory data into a form suitable for "consumption" or processing by our functional or psychological systems—i.e., into information.

The worlds which we could take into account are infinite arrays of ongoing event data. As our eyes and our ears and our minds impose structure, meaningfullness (sic), significance or utility upon those data, the product is information—functional units which our brains are uniquely equipped and "programmed" to process.

Information, not data is the raw material for thinking, decisioning, problem-solving, attitude development, learning and all of the specifically human activities that concern us about our own psychological functioning and the behavior of people. For example, if someone says something to you in your presence (or over the telephone), that person's utterance is potential data for you about an ongoing event of concern to you in your environment. Your sensory equipment translates the physical data of his speech (sound waves) into patterns of neurological data. Those neurological data are then selectively organized and converted into patterns of information. What your friend is actually producing—physical sound waves—is now meaningful to you in the form of consumable or processable messages or bits of intelligence about those particular ongoing events in your external environment.[6]

So the prerequistites of the data to enable them to become information are (a) that they shall be "within the receiver's purview," (b) that they shall be *comprehensible* to the receiver, and (c) that they shall be *validated* by the receiver.[7]

In this process the audit activity may or may not tie in with the *validation* element. The validation may be an informal, automatic procedure, depending on the congruency of the new data with the previously acquired experience. In 999 cases out of 1,000 it is an automatic procedure and not a conscious cognitive process. We arrive at a judgment about the validity of data without a conscious logical process. We may consider the situation as an audit, as we evaluate data against norms—the norms being the norms of our understanding of validity.

In this rudimentary audit, the conscious and purposeful activity resulting in a judgment is missing. If we add to it a purpose—a utility or reason for seeking a judgment or opinion on the validity of the data—we arrive at the concept of the audit.

We may conclude that data can become information without conscious evaluation of their validity. But whenever we make a conscious effort to evaluate the validity of the data, we are *auditing*.

Everybody has exercised audit function on innumerable occasions without recognizing it. Therefore, the study of this function

---

[6]Thayer, pp. 28–29.
[7]*Ibid.*, p. 189.

should not be limited to specialists in a relatively narrow field. It is of interest to every person who wants to have a reliable and realistic idea of the surrounding world and of himself.

DATA, INFORMATION, AND AUDIT

The first evaluation of the data occurs when we perceive them. I hear a crackle in my room. I identify it as the crackling caused by the expansion of the hot-water heating system. I register the notion and go on resting in my bed. I received data, I compared them to a model constructed in the past from cohesive bits of experience and learning, and I stored them away without attaching any importance to it, without seeing any elements of danger in it.

Did I *audit* the data, the crackling noise? Yes, I did. I compared them to the information stored in my memory. I accepted them as a sign representing the top of an information pyramid, consisting of the existence, functioning, and features of our heating system; and I attached it to the existing informations with the remark: "Accepted, OK."

The next day my parents occupied the same room. My mother had no previous experience of crackling in the same room. She heard the noise during the night. She became concerned. She had some experience of similar noises, dating back a few years to when they had moved into a new apartment building. They were the first tenants in the new building, and the workmen had left behind a few tools and a handful of mice. She discovered the mice by the sound they made during the night and by some other physical evidence that clearly indicated their presence. Her conclusions were confirmed when she trapped the mice and got rid of them.

The crackling tied in with this information and contained an element of danger—the undesirable presence of mice! So, immediate action had to be taken! In the morning she told me that we had mice in her room. I asked what made her think so. She communicated data to me: mice in her room. The data did not fit with my previous information stored in my memory. I did not file it, I wanted more details—I audited them. She told me about the noises heard in the room. The crackling was familiar, but it indicated different things to me; it tied in with my information about the heating system. I told her that the noises were caused by the expanding parts of the ducts, and so forth. So I accepted the data—the noises caused by expansion—but rejected the interpretation transmitted by her—the presence of mice—as an error due to her unfamiliarity with the operational details of our house. What I did was clearly audit activity.

But the danger signal triggered by the idea of mice was too strong in her to accept my explanation! She did not believe me. She wanted more convincing evidence than my explanation, and she devised a method of gathering additional evidence.

Without mentioning the matter, she took our cat to her room. She put the cat next to the panel covering the heating elements. The cat was not interested. She kept the cat in the room for an hour or so, until the crackling was heard again. The cat remained calm. My mother accepted as a fact that cats get excited when they sense the traces of mice and start hunting the mice when their presence is heard. The behavior of the cat clearly indicated that the noise was not caused by the mice. An independent expert, with inborn interest and finer senses than we humans have, gave a negative answer to the question "Are mice in the room or not?" She accepted the answer because she trusted the cat. Her audit ended, and she accepted my original explanation.

In this little episode we find all the fundamental elements and concepts of auditing. They are:

1. Interest for a certain purpose, the element of danger. (Are mice present in the room or not?)
2. Broadening of the source area of the data, evoking the data. (Ask me; ask the cat by exposing him to the repeated data.)
3. An opinion, a conclusion, based on the broadened data base.

The interest for audit (the danger element): Every audit has as its purpose the creation of a more or less determinable judgment about the validity, reality, and meaning (interpretation) of certain data. Are the data valid and real? Did she really hear the noises? How do the noises fit in the system of concepts called memory? They were not expected; they were outside the group of information stored in the memory and labeled "normal, no action necessary." They were associated with information labeled "danger, action necessary."

The search for evidence: Evidence is a very broad term, meaning data pertaining to the problem. The same sequence of events may be created, as in laboratory experiments; the data could be of repetitive nature, as in the case of the mysterious noises in my mother's room; or additional data could be perceived by broadening the scope of the observation. Experts who were nearer to the events could be asked. The initially hazy and uncertain model of past events anticipated as reality is refined. Certain elements are confirmed; others are not. Finally, the model becomes more or less objective, that is, it conforms with the judge's (auditor's) own experience or opinion of the segment of events or realities that resulted and remained as residues from previous information. If the evidence allows a judgment about the danger problem (the purpose of the audit), the judgment follows.

The opinion: The judgment or opinion results from the comparison of the model created by the assembly and coordination of evidence and the anticipated "danger type" model of events. It culminates in the opinion (or judgment). No action is necessary if the information that is confirmed warrants no action.

How does our conceptual framework apply to the court activities of the judge? The trial before the judge consists of three basic stages, similar to those established in our previous discussion.

The first step is the stating of the problem. The interest for audit (or danger element) in criminal cases is the prosecutor's claim. The judge or the jury has to decide whether the accused is guilty or not. The danger is that somebody who committed a crime will not be convicted. That would be against social policy and law. The other danger is that an innocent person may be convicted.

The second step is the search for evidence, the establishment of facts, the recreation of events in the mind of the judge. The presentation of evidence is regulated by procedural rules and custom. The parties are bringing the evidence before the court. The judge can add to it only what is known officially by the court. But he has to exercise his opinion (judgment) in many details: what to believe, how to interpret supporting documents and objects, how to explain conflicting statements, who is competent as a witness, what is relevant to the facts or system of events in question. He has to solve the problems "of fact."

When enough evidence has been presented to allow an objective idea on what happened in the area of interest for the application of the model created in the mind of the judge, he will compare it to the different models created by the law, by legislation, and by custom to see where he can establish similarity or identity. He compares the two structures, and his judgment will follow. He solves the "question of law."

Let us consider a third situation from the area of operational auditing.

In the late '40s a young chemist invented a new method of extracting alycin (a substance having value as a drug) from onions, using a simplified process. Using the method worked out in the research laboratories, the costs of production were supposed to be much lower than the previous methods of production. The question was: Will the process work under conditions prevailing in the factory and using the existing equipment?

The production manager ordered the production, using 50 tons of onions as raw material. The equipment was cleaned, the onions were taken into the process, smashed, washed in the recommended solutions, and so on and so forth. The result was that no alycin was produced. All the material, labor, overhead, and time were wasted. The new formula for production was rejected as not workable. The young research chemist invited the production manager, the plant auditor, and the general manager to his laboratories and demonstrated his process. It worked under laboratory conditions. Why did it not work under existing plant conditions?

We know from experience that chemicals react similarly under similar conditions, irrespective of the time. The chemicals are the same and reactions are the same in the first century B.C. and today, that is, if all the other conditions are equal.

Are all conditions equal under laboratory and factory processes? The answer can be given after searching for evidence in the future, if we want to avoid costly experiment and loss of time.

The auditor's task in the actual case was to broaden the information base. He had to divide the whole production process into small comparable sections. He could not afford to experiment with 1,000 tons of onions. His only resource was to build a smaller model of the factory's production equipment. In the laboratory the crushing was done in porcelain pots with glass bars. In the factory the production equipment was copper lined, and the crushing was done by steel rollers and bars. He asked the chemist to use copper pots and steel in the laboratory. The onion pulp produced was further handled by the usual laboratory equipment. Alycin was still obtained but in smaller quantities. After the next step of production, using small-sized model pieces of the factory equipment, the alycin disappeared in the laboratory experiment. The conclusion: The chemical process was different in copper-lined and steel equipment and in glass-lined equipment. The process could not work with the existing equipment of the factory. Other types of pots, rollers, pipes, and so forth were needed. The new type of equipment was too expensive at the given moment, and therefore the plans to use the new process were abandoned. Is this type of activity an audit? Does it fit our definition?

Where is the element of information or data? We see a plan, an organization or sequence of activities—the process worked out by the young chemist. We have to evaluate it against a norm: Will it work in the future? Will it work under certain changed conditions? We have to create the norms against which we will match the existing data, and we have to create evidence that will be valid in the future. So it is an audit activity.

If we compare the three examples discussed above, we can see similarities and differences. The similarities (an interest created by some danger) are: not to eliminate the mice in the first example, not to convict an innocent person in the second, and not to succeed with a plan of action in the third. My mother created present evidence for her evaluations in the first case; the judge evaluated evidence of past happenings in the second; and in the third case, we had to create norms of the future, which we were able to do only by assuming that present evidence would be valid in the future.

The three examples illustrate the three types of audit activities in their relationship to the flow of time:

(a) The contemporary (present) audit,

(b) The historical (retrospective) audit, and

(c) The anticipatory (future) audit.

The classification will be of importance in our discussion of audit procedures.

THE POSTULATES OF AUDITING

The first step in the process of data becoming evidence is the apprehension or receipt of the data. Next, we validate the data and evaluate them in the light of our experience before we accept them as information.

What is the difference between this process and the process that we defined as "audit"?

Purpose (goal). The first difference is that the audit has a purpose. The scope and nature of evidence to be collected, considered, or created, the norms (criteria) against which the evidence will be evaluated, and the opinion or judgment derived as a result—all depend on the purpose of the audit.

We cannot prove that every audit has to have a purpose. It is a basic postulate of auditing; it is evident; and, therefore, it has to be accepted. The process in which data become information has no specific purpose. We may assume that the capacity of apprehension (the capacity of receiving data and the ability to store and use information) has the general purpose of enabling us to function as intelligent living creatures and adapt to our surroundings. But data do not create a purpose. If we seek and select data for a specific purpose—for example, to allow a judgment or opinion on their validity and relevance—we are entering the domain of auditing.

My mother has as a purpose to determine the presence or absence of mice. The judge has as a purpose for his activities the administration of justice—the conviction or acquittal of the accused. The operational auditor has as his purpose the necessity to determine why something that succeeded under laboratory conditions did not work in the factory.

There is no audit without purpose. The purpose gives the necessary unity for the evidence to be gathered or provided, for the norms to be used in the evaluation process, and for the judgment or opinion to complete the concept of the audit. It is the unifying postulate for the other components of the audit concept.

Judgment (opinion). The actual situation determining the purpose of the audit activity calls for an intermediate or final decision, which necessitates a judgment or opinion. We use the terms judgment and opinion as *synonymous*. (Although for our purpose the two concepts can be treated as identical, there is a difference between the two terms: Opinion is a belief or conclusion held with confidence. If the person having the opinion has an authority to exercise his opinion, or if some formal proceedings preceded the utterance of an opinion, we speak about judgment. Belief is the mental acceptance of a phenomenon or proposition as true, valid, or real.)

The judgment refers back to the purpose of the audit. It consists of a comparison, a synoptic view of the model or models created in the mind of the judge, with a norm or system of norms and a conclusion arrived at by the comparison.

The judgment could be communicated by the judge to the other members of the society, or it may be kept by the judge for himself. We can have an audit for ourselves without communicating our opinion, but we cannot audit without arriving at an opinion. If we are unable to gather evidence, we have no audit at all and we cannot arrive at an opinion by this mental process. We may have a belief.

We have to apply the negative test in order to determine the existence of a postulate in the search for its existence. Is an audit possible or thinkable without an opinion or judgment? The answer is no. Without arriving at an opinion, we are searching for an audit; we try to establish the audit process, but our activity is unorganized. There is only an attempt to audit.

Evidence. To be able to have an opinion we must have a model, a system of phenomena or representations and a system of norms. The forming of an opinion results as a comparison of the two component parts. The ability to have an opinion is the ability to see similarities, identity, and differences or incongruities between the two conceptual sets. We build the conceptual model of phenomena by gathering or accepting evidence. Without evidence there cannot be an opinion, and therefore there is no audit. We have to accept as a postulate that evidence—past, present, or anticipated—is required for an audit. We thus arrive at the *postulate of evidence.*

The other component in the judgment is the system of norms against which we compare the set derived from the evidence. Opinion, or judgment, is unthinkable without a system of criteria (norms). In our daily life the most often used system of norms is that of reality or validity. The system of norms has to be established and accepted in order to enable us to arrive at an opinion. It is a postulate of auditing, as it is also a postulate for the concept of opinion.

Norms (criteria). The postulate of norms is the fourth of the basic assumptions that we have to accept as granted. Can we imagine auditing without the norms existing for the purpose of the opinion or judgment in the mind of the judge?

We have to accept without proof that the norms (criteria) exist in our thinking. We see only the effect of the norms in the acts, writings, or verbal utterances of other individuals, and we can arrive at the concept by analyzing our own thinking. The judgments—such as good, bad, nice—are unthinkable without the assumption of an underlying standard of values (norms) which are implicit in the quality judgments, just as the unit of measurement is needed if we want to express an opinion as the result of the measurement process.

Communication. Postulates are cornerstones on which we will build our inquiry and the structure of principles. Their number could be multiplied, as we could go deeper and deeper into the analysis of human mind and intellect. But we have to leave the rest of the postulates to the disciplines of philosophy and psychology. We have to accept that human beings can think, act, and understand, that the past can be remembered and communicated to us within our memory and by others. We have to accept that the world exists and that we are able to change it. But one other postulate is of primary importance to the audit concept: the *postulate of communication.*

The postulate of communication asserts that communication of data to individuals by their memory and by the outside world exists and that it is meaningful. The existence, the validity, and the interpretation of these data are the subject matter of the audit process. Without them no understanding, evaluation, or judgment would be possible. In keeping in mind this relationship of the postulate of communication to the postulates of purpose, opinion, evidence, and norms, we can examine the relationship of auditing to the general theory of communication. I hope it will be a useful field to investigate.

Our conclusions: (1) Human actions exist, and human beings can have a purpose for their actions. The concept of purpose exists and has an influence on human intelligence (postulate of purpose). (2) Human opinion (judgment) exists and is communicable (postulate of opinion or judgment, postulate of communicaton). (3) Evidence exists, and its retrieval or transmittal by data is possible (postulate of evidence, postulate of communication). (4) The system of norms (criteria) is used in statements, opinions, and judgments; and although it is only an abstraction, it exists because it enables us to make a statement, opinion, or judgment.

THE QUALITIES OF POSTULATES

The postulates have to possess certain qualities in order to perform their useful functions within the framework of a theory. "Every proposition in the system must cohere, in conceptual structure with the rest" (*coherence*).[8]

It is evident that the proposed postulates belong to the system of auditing knowledge as in fact they are derived from the definition of auditing. The postulate of communications is the only one that does not follow directly from the definition. In our definition we implied that communication exists and that it is possible. This concept is the connecting link between information theory and auditing, and perhaps it will be useful to explore and explain it later in more detail.

The postulate has to contribute to further inquiry (*contributiveness*). "The work postulate" is ordinarily applied to premises for deduction.[9] We will derive our audit principles from our postulates.

---

[8] S. K. Langer, *An Introduction to Symbolic Logic*, 2nd ed. (New York: Dover Publications, Inc., 1953), p. 185.
[9] *Ibid.*

The third required quality of postulates is *consistency.* "Two propositions which contradict each other, that is, which cannot both be true, can never be admitted to the same system." [10] There is no inconsistency between the coexistence of the concepts of purpose, judgment, norms, evidence, and communication. They complement each other to form the concept of audit. They are not contradicting each other, so our system created by them is not illogical.

The fourth criterion is *independence.* If a proposition is deductible from one of the postulates already given, then it is a theorem, a necessary fact, not another assumption. The fact that we "assume" rather than "prove" it to ourselves is a purely psychological circumstance which has no bearing on the logical status of a proposition; if it might be proved, it is a theorem, and to regard it as a postulate is simply an error. Fortunately, this error is not serious, since deductions made from a theorem are exactly as good as those made from a postulate. If we regard a theorem as a postulate and think ourselves to have one more arbitrary assumption than in fact we have, then we merely do not know how nice our system is. [11] We may ask some questions when we consider our five postulates in the light of the above criterion: Is not the existence of the concept of norms inherent to the postulate of judgment? Is not the concept of evidence inherent to the concept of communication? We may prove that judgment implies the existence of norms and data, and we may argue that we could prove the possibility of evidence from the concept of communication. To answer these questions we have to push further in the theory of communication and clarify the relationship of communication theory to our established postulates of auditing.

THEOREM OF COMMUNICATION

Our purpose is to enquire into the theory of auditing in its relationship to communication (information) theory. Among the postulates of auditing, we listed the postulate of communication as having an important role in the audit function. We will not stop at this level and simply accept that communication does exist.

[10] *Ibid.*
[11] *Ibid.*, p. 186.

We have to push farther and analyze the communication concept. We want to establish the postulate of communication as theorem and not as a postulate for the purposes of audit theory.

What is "communication"? Professor Lee Thayer selected four definitions "more or less at random" from the many definitions used and going around:

1. Communication is the process of effecting an interchange of understanding between two or more people.
2. Communication is the mutual interchange of ideas by any effective means.
3. ". . . The imparting or interchange of thoughts, opinions, or information by speech, writing, or signs" (*American College Dictionary*).
4. Communication is the arrangement of environmental stimuli to produce certain desired behavior on the part of the organism.[12]

Professor Thayer justly rejects the above definitions on the following grounds:

a. Communication is not an "intentional" process. The communicator may attempt to "control" the conditions of communication, but it is evident that the control may or may not be efficient and present.
b. The definitions imply "too much rationality and conscious awareness." "People react to far more than words or symbols as such."
c. Communication is not something that we can turn on or turn off. Communication is a continuous function of human beings.[13]

Without repeating the thorough description and analysis of the basic phenomena of communication and its role in the life of individuals, groups, and organizations, we may attempt to define communication as a "human process of receiving stimuli (data),

[12] Thayer, p. 13.
[13] *Ibid.*

transforming them into information, memory, and the ability to generate stimuli (data) accordingly."[14]

From our attempted definitions, we can derive the following postulates:

a. Postulate of stimuli (data): Stimuli, or data, exist. We cannot prove them. They are evident.

b. Postulate of memory: We can remember past stimuli (data) and information generated by them.

c. Postulate of information: We transform stimuli (data) into information. We may call it also the postulate of intelligence. It is a basic truth. It is evident. Tools of this process are the concepts and causality, the instruments of human thinking.

d. Postulate of data emission: We produce data (stimuli) for other receivers. The existence of data produced by us is evident. We cannot deny reception of data attributed to ourselves.

It is needless to point out that we live in a world that is recreated by our intelligence as information from data (stimuli) is supplied and attributed by us to the surrounding world. Our idea about the world is created by the attributes generated by data (stimuli) that we have received.

The connecting link between the audit process and the broad, general field of communication is the *theorem of communication* (which is not a postulate, as we called it earlier in order to simplify our presentation).

[14] *Ibid.*

CHAPTER II

AUDIT STRUCTURE
(THE AUDIT MODEL)

WE PUT THE AUDIT PROCESS under the magnifying glass, and we found that it consists of a chain of interdependent judgments or decisions. The first one is the selection of norms (decision model) that will achieve the purpose (goals) of the audit.

What is the purpose (or objective) of the Statutory Audit of the Shareholders Auditor? Under the Canada Corporations Act, his objectives are to establish that the financial statements present fairly the financial position of the client corporation.

Because we may question whether traditional financial statements do or do not present the financial position of a business, we add as additional qualification the words "in accordance with accepted accounting principles."

In this case the purpose itself is defined with reference to two distinct sets of norms:

(a) The words "present fairly" imply that the objects or object (in this case, the financial position) presented is supposed to be existing and true.

(b) The second set of norms referred to is "financial statements . . . in accordance with accepted accounting principles." Those requirements indicate that the "truth" (or "reality"), established under (a), has to be presented in a special form, established under (b).

The audit for "truth" or "validity" is very common in life. I called it "basic audit"; perhaps we could call it "verification," as the root of this expression contains the Latin adjective *verus*, that is, "true."

The verification or basic audit may be an audit in itself if the purpose of an audit is to establish the truth alone. But it is not only an independent evaluation; it also has a very important role within each evaluation process in the acceptance or rejection of the purported evidence.

In the audit for truth, we use reality (or, better said, our own concept of reality) as the norm (or criteria). Reality, as it exists in our intellect, is a complex system of schemata, the sublimation of past experiences that we learned from early childhood to distinguish from the "nontruth" or "not real."

So the shareholders auditor has to perform certain procedures in order to establish the truth of the purported evidence presented by the records of the company.

If there were no purported evidence and the purpose of the evaluation were the establishment of evidence, we would talk about investigation.

At the moment we have to skip over the theory of audit procedures for establishing the evidence; we can only state that once the model of evidence is established, it passes a judgment, a secondary judgment within the framework of the original main evaluation process. In this secondary judgment, the auditor arrives at the conclusion that the evidence is "true," "true with modifications," "not true," or "not existing." If the evidence is "not existing," the audit—the evaluation process—comes to an end. Without evidence (past, present or future), we cannot arrive at any other final conclusions than to deny an opinion or judgment.

If the purported evidence is "true," it is verified; and we have to pass to the second subjudgment: we have to match our verified "evidence model" to the norms of presentation according to accepted accounting principles.

The categories, or pigeonholes, in the "presentation norm system" are organized according to the goals, the purpose of the audit. They are: "presented fairly," "fairly with qualifications (that is, with modifications)," or "not presented fairly."

The auditor or the judge has to transform the truth model in the form required by the structure of norms used in order to be able to perform the synopsis, the judgment. The true, verified data base is organized, classified, and summarized according to the requirements set by the norms. In other terms, the data pyramid is adjusted to fit the classification and disclosure requirements set by the norms of financial statements according to "accepted accounting principles."

In the synopsis the auditor arrives at his conclusion.

The next step is the expression of his judgment in the audit report. The report, the "auditor's opinion," is the final product that can serve as source data by the parties to whom it is directed for their information purposes. Unfortunately, as it is presented in a non-vanishing form—writing—it can be used also by parties to whom it was not directed and who may not be aware of the goals of the evaluation process.

The "Structure of the Statutory Audit" is pictured in Figure 3.

I have attempted to show the evaluation process under a magnifying glass. It is a question of terminology whether we identify the evaluation process and the audit process. (It depends on the problem of anticipatory evidence. Is an audit using anticipatory evidence audit or not audit?)

The resulting picture shows the component parts of the audit process as a series of interrelated judgments. But outside the component parts shown, there is a whole area of tremendous importance to the theory of auditing: the problem of communication.

The communication problem permeates the whole field and therefore the theory of auditing. We have to perceive the purpose of the audit usually from groups of data presented by others. The norms, the evidence, and the purported evidence are groups of data. They have to be perceived and interpreted; inferences have to be drawn from them. The audit findings have to be communicated.

In Figures 4, 5, and 6, we present the conceptual framework of our three examples mentioned earlier in our book. It will be useful to have a more rigorous look at them.

In our first example (noises in our bedroom indicating presence of mice), the purpose (goal) of the audit was to establish the presence of mice, unwanted guests. The norms (criteria) applied were those of "reality." The purported evidence was the belief of my mother, an inference made from perceiving crackling noises during the night. She applied audit procedures: She used an expert on mice (the cat) to conduct an inquiry and, from the behavior of the cat, she arrived at the adjusted evidence. The adjusted-evidence model indicated that the noises were not caused by mice.

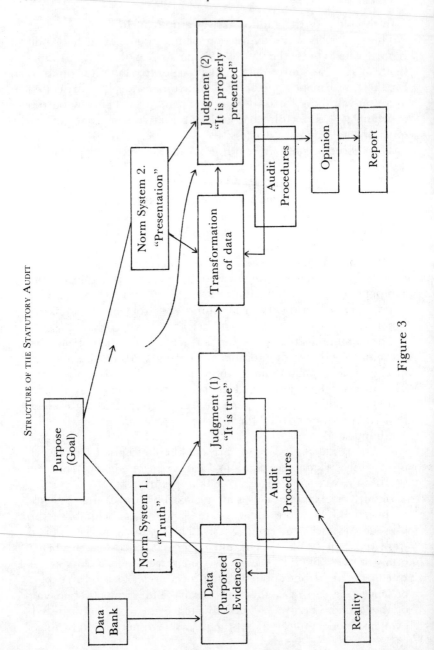

STRUCTURE OF THE STATUTORY AUDIT

Figure 3

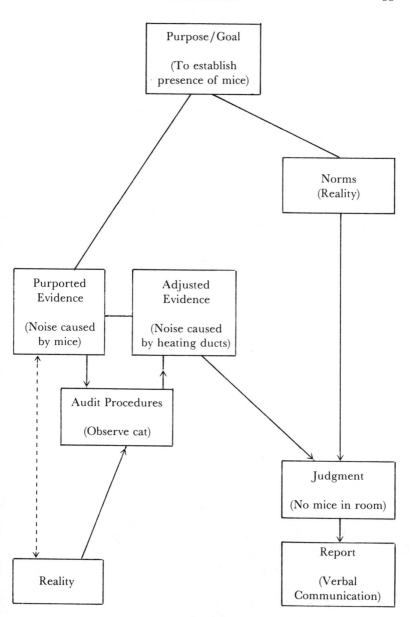

Figure 4

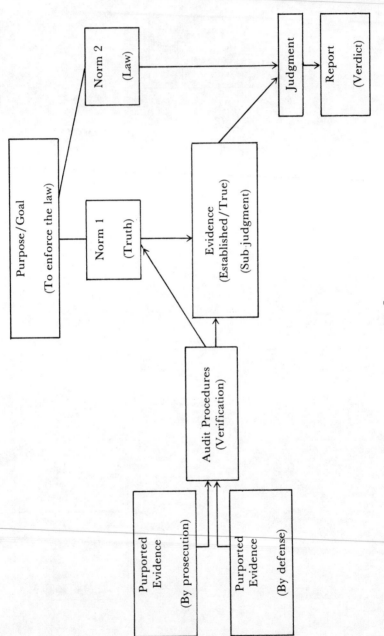

Figure 5

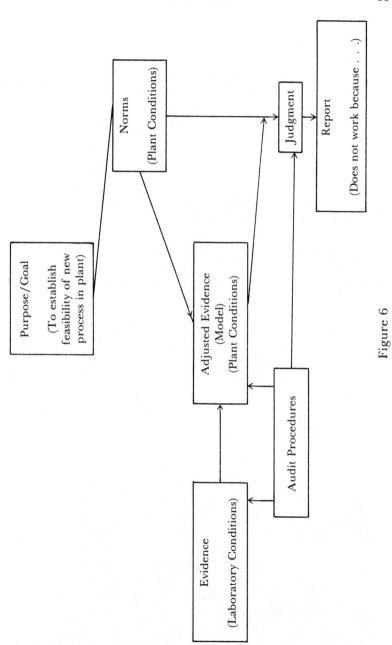

Figure 6

Thereupon, she arrived at the conclusion (judgment, opinion) that there were no mice in the room. Figure 4 serves as an illustration for the process.

In the second example, the conceptual structure of the judgment procedure that is followed by the judge is relatively simple. The procedures are and were so important that they are highly formalized by historical traditions and statutory regulations.

The purpose of the judge is to enforce the law. The two systems of norms applied are: (1) reality, or truth; and (2) the system of criminal offenses as defined by the Criminal Code.

The prosecution presents the purported evidence. The defense questions it or presents its own version of evidence.

In establishing the truth, the judge verifies the presentations by applying audit procedures.

After establishing the true evidence in a form suitable for matching it against the system of the Criminal Code, the judge arrives at his judgment—guilty or not guilty in one or several of the offenses.

He then communicates his judgment in the verdict or, we may say, in his report.

Figure 5 illustrates the conceptual structure of the process.

The flow chart of our third case presents more difficulties. Here the purpose of the procedures was to find out why a process that was successful under laboratory (lab.) conditions did not work under factory (plant) conditions.

The norms (criteria) were the "process under plant conditions."

The existing evidence was the "process under lab. conditions."

The operational auditor had to break down the process into smaller units, into operations within one piece of production equipment. It was economically prohibitive to observe the operations by the use of the actual plant equipment. The auditor had to build an exact replica of the machinery (models) for use in his tests. Actually he attempted to adjust the evidence to fit the conditions of the "norm system." He then applied audit procedures (observation of the individual phases of production) and tests (chemical analysis) to the processes by unit of production.

His tests led him to the explanation of why the process worked under laboratory conditions but not under plant conditions.

Actually he transformed the evidence available into another model of the evidence which was closer to the "norm system"—the plant conditions. With his audit procedures he concentrated on the transformation of evidence models.

We may visualize the component parts of the whole process in Fig. 6.

CHAPTER III
THE PSYCHOLOGY OF INFORMATION

FOR A SIMPLE ILLUSTRATION of the conceptual framework within the communication process, the trivial sequence of "data-receiver-information-storage-decision-action" is satisfactory. But in its conceptual simplicity it is very far removed from reality.

Information can be created only by living individuals. Data can be handled in a certain pattern, stored and displayed in print, sound, or pictures, in records, and/or in mechanical and electronic devices. But those data are not information.

The individual is exposed to an infinite variety and number of potential data: everything that is within the scope of reception of his sensory organs. We may hear, see, feel, and smell data. Everything "could" exist for us; the whole universe is an infinite, concurrently active potential source of data. Our sensory organs shelter us from the universe of data by admitting only those within the limits of our perceptions, a relatively small range. And even from the data concurrently perceived by us, we allow only one or two to enter into our "inner world."

This inner world, our "conscious personality," is a special feature of the human and animal beings. We have a capacity to remember some effects of the data perceived, to recall and remember them "in our memory."

The data perceived by our sight form a picture in our inner world. The picture may be immediately forgotten as a whole, but some component elements may attach or accrue to memories of pictures organized in a certain way. Some signs, either in isolation or in a certain set (such as signals, words, and sentences), may evoke pictures, series of pictures, or ideas that are very different from the visual surroundings in which we originally focused on the signs. We recognize the signs, and we attribute something to them: a special message. We say that the data were understood and not just received by us. The data passed the threshold of our sensory capacities; in addition they also passed the intellectual threshold of our inner world and became understood in a certain way.

Our inner world is the function of our memory, and it is organized in sets of images, ideas, concepts, feelings, and opinions that are arrived at or accepted during the whole span of our life. The organized structures contain, not the data, but information, as the data become information when they pass the intellectual threshold and are accepted or rejected, evaluated, and classified by the individual understanding them.

The organized structures of information are called "schemata" in the psychological literature.[1]

According to Bartlett's definition: "*Schema is an active organization of past reactions or of past experiences which must always be supposed to be operating in any well adapted organic response.*"[2]

The schemata are sets, patterns, or models in which the elements of our memory are organized; the elements of our memory are not data but are systems of concepts, opinions, or events constructed from data by experience and learning.

THE STRUCTURE OF DATA AND RELATED CONCEPTS

Data are isolated from the surrounding world by our sensory organs. They are sensed or felt as differences in the world around us. Usually they occur in sets. In a picture (in visual sensation) some forms or bodies move as a unit. In hearing, some sounds follow each other in the same continuous pattern on several occasions. As children we had to learn to speak: to learn that the same sequence of sounds resulted in the attention of a person whose presence was nice and comforting. Human persons are born with an inherent urge to be active and to exercise their facilities, so we try our best to get the attention of our society by trying to show off with our ability to express ourselves. Later

[1] See F. C. Bartlett, *Thinking* (London: Allen & Unwin, 1958).
[2] *Ibid.*, p. 158.

we learn to read and write. We get used to accepting words as something existing, as concepts. Due to the impact of the language, our memory and imagination are organized in concepts, in wordlike sets of the world around us.

We are exposed to data, and the resulting information takes the form of concepts, events, and opinions through interpretation and inferences.

When data pass the inner threshold of our intellect, they are interpreted by us, and we draw inferences from them.

To *interpret*, in the sense that we use it, means "to clarify the meaning of a message, to elucidate, to expound the significance of a message or of data."[3] *Inference*, however, is a conclusion that is arrived at by reasoning or implications.

The two concepts overlap and are related to each other. *Interpretation* of the data consists of an enrichment of the data by fitting it into different schemata. It is an extremely complex intellectual process. Data are recognized as such and are organized into sets or concepts; and the sets, or models, are compared and fitted into schemata which are emerging in our conscious memory.

Inference is the consequence of interpretation, of a further enrichment of data by elements of our experience, and of knowledge contained in the schema, the mental structure with which the interpretation associated the set of data.

Every elementary text on sensory psychology deals with the interrelationship of the "object"-"image on retina"-"information." We may attempt to show the interpretation process in the sequence in Figure 7.

We may infer from Information I that the house is occupied by new owners; from Information II that the inhabitants are not rich; and from III that the house is occupied by a small family.

The concepts, the results of interpretation, evoke memories of opinions or events by inference; and the events or opinions evoke other concepts, depending on the organization of schemata within the individual. Each sensation or event evokes a whole array of information, and each piece of information may evoke an array of possible inferences.

[3] Meaning adapted from *The American Heritage Dictionary of the English Language*, ed. W. Morris (New York: American Heritage Publishing Co., 1969).

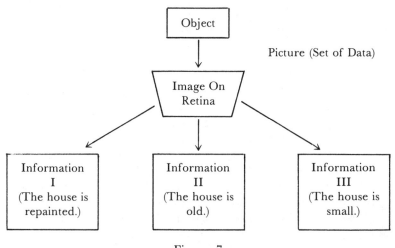

Figure 7

MEMORY, CONCEPTS, AND WORDS

We perceive the world around us and our memory as existing and determined in space and time. We sense the space through our eyes and ears and by feeling our movements in the space. We can change the pictures surrounding us by changing our place in them. We reduce distances by touching and moving things.

The original impulses or stimuli that are perceived produce an "echo effect."

Although we cannot reproduce the stimuli or impulses, we can recall the data that we received; we can remember their effect in our inner world, in our memory. We remember past events and pictures, although certain parts of the events, pictures, and sounds are missing from the recall. Our memory can be controlled to a certain extent, but sometimes events or pictures "pop up" unintentionally without control: our memory is semi-independent. With time and in competition with the constantly emerging new stimuli or data, our capacity to recall certain events or pictures disappears; we forget. The echoes left by past sensations fade away.

The data perceived in space and time sometimes display certain features that are repeating themselves: some data are constant in their relationship to each other in space and time. They may be moving together in sets; they appear in similar combinations, or one set of data is always followed by another set. The data appearing in more or less constant configurations or sets were considered units in the unorganized array of the world around us. As concepts they become objects and persons—the units of thinking in our inner world.

The sequence of sets in time generates the causality, the relationship of cause and effect as a concept generated by experience.

The data are perceived by us in passing our intellectual threshold as signifying concepts. They may be recalled in their "echo" effect as pictures, sounds, or their sequences. But pictures, sounds, and events get connected to concepts. If they are attached to concepts, they lose their identity in space and time, but our capacity to recall them increases. Concepts do not fade away so fast. They remain longer in our inner world. With the help of the structure of concepts—the schema—we salvage the pictures, sounds, and events in our memory, although in a poorer form: some details are lost; some are not taken into the conceptual framework.

In communicating with humans we use words as signals for concepts, and we organize words in sentences, in opinions, and in statements.

The person who is listening to us and understanding the language that we use is already conditioned or programmed to interpret the groups of data as concepts, opinions, and statements because he learned to use the same language and concepts.

MEANING

Most of the human communications use words structured in sentences as tools for the process. The words are supposed to have a meaning or meanings.

The words do not represent objects or relationships between objects as perceived by our sensory organs. They are signs and labels. They have no objective identity. In addition, they are by necessity generalizations at a higher or lower level.

Alfred Korzybski, in his *Science and Sanity*, introduced the term "semantic reaction" to indicate an individual's capacity to understand and interpret the meanings of words and sentences. (The term "semantic" is derived from the Greek verb "semainein," to signify, to mean.) I quote from *Science and Sanity:* "All effective and psychological responses to words and other stimuli involving meanings are to be considered as semantic reactions."[4]

The semantic reactions of an individual depend on his previous experience, his knowledge of the terms used in the message, his emotional state, and his relationship to the sender.

We could identify the semantic reactions of the humans with the "conditional reflexes." Words and statements evoke a certain state of understanding, which is colored by a certain emotional effect in an individual.

Semantic blindness, or aphasia, makes communications impossible.

S. I. Hayakawa, in *Language in Thought and Action*, writes about the importance of the circumstances (context) as determinants of "meaning" as follows:

> The ignoring of contexts in any act of interpreta-
> tion(—and in consequence in inferences made) is at
> best a stupid practice. At its worst, it can be a vicious
> practice. A common example is the sensationalistic
> newspaper story in which a few words by a public
> personage are torn out of their context and made the
> basis of a completely misleading account. There is the
> incident of a Veteran's Day speaker, a university teacher,
> who declared before a high school assembly that the
> Gettysburg Address was a "powerful piece of propagan-
> da." The context clearly revealed that "propaganda"
> was used not according to its popular meaning, but
> rather, as the speaker himself stated, to mean "explaining
> the moral purposes of a war." The context also revealed
> that the speaker was a great admirer of Lincoln.
> However, the local newspaper, ignoring the context,
> presented the account in such a way as to suggest that
> the speaker had called Lincoln a liar. On this basis the
> newspaper began a campaign against the instructor.

[4] A. Korzybski, *Science and Sanity*, 4th ed. (Lakeville, Conn.: The International Non-Aristotelian Library Publishing Co., 1958), p. 25.

The speaker remonstrated with the editor of the newspaper, who replied, in effect: "I don't care what else you said. You said the Gettysburg Address was propaganda, didn't you?" This appeared to the editor complete proof that Lincoln had been maligned and that the speaker deserved to be discharged from his position at the university.

Similar practices may be found in advertisements. A reviewer may be quoted on the jacket of a book as having said, "A brilliant work," while reading of the context may reveal that what he really said was, "It just falls short of being a brilliant work." There are some people who will always be able to find a defense for such a practice in saying, "But he did use the words 'A brilliant work,' didn't he?"[5]

CLUES

We think of a clue as anything that guides or directs in the solution of a problem or mystery.

Groups of data are identified with concepts and are fitted into existing schemata by the receiver, according to certain clues that facilitate the connection of the data to the schemata. Clues are the elements assisting the receiver in the interpretation of the group of data received. We may try to classify the clues as follows:

1. Clues originating in the source of the data:
   a. The relationship between the source of data and the receiver
   b. Previous communications
   c. Circumstances surrounding the communication process
2. Clues originating in the data or group of data:
   a. The way the data are transmitted by the media ("The media is the message," M. McLuhan)
   b. The grouping, the organization of the data
   c. The intensity and tone of the data

[5] S. I. Hayakawa, *Language in Thought and Action*, 3rd ed. (New York: Harcourt, Brace, Jovanovich, Inc., 1972), pp. 56–67.

3. Clues originating in the receiver:
   a. The importance attached to the data
   b. The physical and mental state of the receiver
   c. The competition of other data
   d. The knowledge and experience of the receiver.

The above classification is certainly not complete; it is just an attempt to indicate this complicated area of human psychology.

Clues are guidelines in the interpretation of the data and help the receiver to make the inferences by indicating or evoking the appropriate schemata in his inner world. They are not "inborn" to an individual but are acquired by experience and by exposure to chains of events following the reception of similar groups or types of data. They can also be acquired by learning, although the ability of utilizing clues learned without experiencing them fades away if they are not carried over to practice and are not strengthened by experience. The development of certain and predeterminable clues is the purpose of education and training and of the present work on the theory of evaluation and judgment.

In a mechanical or electronic data-storage and -display apparatus, the data are stored if the impulses are of the proper, narrowly determined character. They may be stored, transformed, and so forth, but the device has no clues and cannot produce information. The ability to interpret the data and to make inferences is missing. Mechanical or electronic devices have no ability to have clues. The clues in them are replaced by the program and the instruction: how to handle the data. Humans can be programmed, too, by training and experience. But no training and experience can shut out all possible schemata and the eventuality of the development of new clues.

ATTITUDES

A multitude of schemata coexist in the intellect, the inner world of an individual. They can be controlled to a certain extent. They are influenced by the physical and emotional state of the individual. Circumstances outside the person's control may have an impact on them. We may call them sets of interlocking concepts which are changing and automatically *restructuring themselves.*

When I hear the crackling sound in my room, I receive a set

of data. I interpret them as noise (a concept) created by the expanding ducts (concept). I infer from it that the warm-water heating is working. No action is needed.

My mother receives the same set of data. She interprets them as a noise (concept) created by mice (concept). She infers from this that mice are present in the room. She wants action.

My father did not receive the data; he was asleep. No interpretation; no inferences.

The "attitudes" of an individual are more or less constant within a short period of time. This system of values, individual goals, and physical and mental conditions will usually not change from moment to moment.

Groups of people living in the same time, adopting the same values, and possessing the same inborn temperament and knowledge—which are all absorbed from daily contact with each other—will have more or less the same semantic reactions to data, and they will have similar attitudes. The reliance on the unchanging constant qualities of the attitudes allows us to rely on the reactions evoked by a message or a series of messages. If we misjudge the attitude of the persons we are dealing with, our communication will not be successful, and our planning and decision-making processes will prove disastrous. In the prediction model we have to anticipate the human reactions to the predicted or expected events. Therefore, the attitudes have to be investigated, if possible, to reduce the risk of failure.

We can learn about the attitudes of our fellow men only from their acts and statements (judgments). The acts again can be interpreted as the results of certain opinions and judgments.

The attitudes can be researched and investigated if we are in the possession of enough reliable evidence. We have to point out that past and present attitudes may be known, but attitudes change with changing conditions and time; therefore, governments, administrators, and managers attempt to control or influence the attitudes and semantic reactions of individuals.

Advertising, propaganda, political campaigns, the actions of the not-hidden persuaders, educators, and so forth, are some of the instances that have as a purpose the change of semantic reactions and attitudes.

The purpose of the present book is also to change the attitudes of the reader by opening up channels of hitherto nonexisting relationships, thereby creating new semantic reactions and insights and rearranging existing schemata.

THE INFERENCE OF VALIDITY

The most common inference drawn by the receiver of the data is that of their validity. We have an inherent ability—a tendency—to pass a judgment or opinion on the validity of the message received after data are interpreted. We call this procedure "the basic audit" because the receiver of the data evaluates the contents of the message, as is indicated by his interpreting the data against his ideas on their truth and validity, and he passes a judgment on it.

The data have to pass a third threshold in the individual. The first threshold is that of the sensory organs; the second is the interpretation of the data (the understanding); and the third is the acceptance or rejection of the contents of the data following the basic audit.

The interpretation of data is an opinion or judgment on the meaning of the data received. An opinion is the result of the synoptic view in our inner world of the data in their environment and of the concepts organized in schemata in our imagination. From our past experience we have established a system of concepts, a model of the world that has the quality of being valid, of being true. In the interpretation process we use an established system of concepts as norms. The data received have to be grouped so that they fit into the existing framework of concepts. This is a procedure by trial and error, using the clues as guidelines. If the group of data under similar circumstances was experienced by the receiver, familiar clues will help to fit the data, as symbols of well-known concepts, into the existing system of concepts, into the schemata. If they are valid, they add nothing to the content of the schemata. They just confirm the validity of the schemata by adding to them the element of recent occurrence.

I possess a set of concepts, an opinion based on past experience, namely, that the heating elements in my room crackle if the heating system is operating.

Data are perceived while I am in the room, and they originate in the direction of the heating elements. They are grouped so that they recall the quality of sounds experienced on previous occasions. I can fit the group of data (the clues) into the framework of concepts (the schemata) existing in my memory. There is a complete correspondence: the crackling sound is created by the expansion of the ducts. I passed an opinion. I compared evidence (the new set of data) and norms (a system of concepts that is considered valid), and I found complete correspondence. I did not know that the heating system was operating. By passing an opinion on the sensation of crackling sounds, I inferred that the hot-water heating system was working. *Interpretation* is an opinion on the groups of data and their connection to concepts or schemata existing in our memory. *Inference* is a further judgment, an extension of the information drawn from comparing schemata, or structures of concepts, with each other.

In my memory an old opinion or judgment was stored away: The heating system makes crackling noises when it operates. I hear crackling noises; therefore, the heating system is operating.

In logic we would say that we followed the rules of deductive reasoning. In the theory of communication and psychology, taking into consideration the structure of human thinking processes, we say: We inferred from a message a situation using information remembered.

My mother interpreted the same group of data differently. Her interpretation was that the noise was caused by mice gnawing on wood. Her inference from this interpretation: Mice are in the room; therefore, action is needed.

I questioned the validity of her interpretation of the data and, with it, her conclusions, her inferences. I considered them invalid, not true. Why? What did I do?

I compared her interpretation of the noise to my previous experience with the same type of noise experienced at different times in the same location. I had an established opinion on my judgment, namely, that it is valid, or true.

First of all, what is validity? What is reality?

Valid is an expression, a sign. It represents several concepts and has several meanings, as we will see later. In the sense used by us now, it signifies "real, sound, supportable by evidence."

Reality is the quality of being existent, having the state of actuality.

In judging my mother's interpretation of the data, I used as evidence her statement on the noises, her description of the circumstances under which her data were received, and her interpretation of the data. I used as comparison the norms (criteria) of validity and reality, and I arrived at the conclusion that her interpretation was invalid.

So there are norms, the norms of validity and reality, against which schemata resulting from interpretation of data and inferences are compared by the individual unconsciously or consciously, thereby auditing the interpretation of data and the inferences drawn.

The information resulting from the interpretation of the data may be true, probable, improbable, impossible, or untrue in its relationship to the norm of reality.

Reality is a feeling established by experience. All human beings are capable of remembering the component parts of the outside and inside world, with a special tag attached to certain information, labeling them as valid under all known circumstances, as perhaps valid, and as not valid or not true. The lack of the ability by a person or a society to establish this norm of validity or reality would be considered by others, who have the ability to see the norm, as a mental disorder, with the result being the destruction of the individual or the society. Perhaps it is established as a result of the continuity of sensations and the capacity to test our information about the surrounding world by evoking data through different sensory organs.

If somebody who does not have the ability to feel and experience the norm of validity or reality is refrained from every action, he or she may survive as a vegetable. The importance of norms is predominant in the second phase of the information process, in the use of information for inferences and for action.

New data will be judged or audited in the light of the norms or criteria of validity and reality, and they will be integrated in the existing schemata of the memory. If actions are considered, their relationship to the norms of validity, reality, or desired events is of primary importance. Human beings have the capacity to establish norms in order to comply with the surrounding world. But this capacity to establish norms is not limited to the validity or realities of the surrounding world. We are able to create the imaginary norm of a so-called material reality which surrounds us. We perceive our memory, our store of information, and our feeling of ourselves as being just as "material" as the outside world is. Very early in our lives, due to the social milieu that we are born into, we learn to develop patterns for action and thinking initially by imitation only. We develop special information as norms, against which we have to compare our planned actions or ways of actions. The norms like "Baby cries; baby gets attention" are special operational schemata. They get more complicated as the baby grows. Finally, with age, the norms, as information not only for thinking but also for feeling, create a structure similar to that of a skeleton for our behavior. We have them, and we cannot get away from them. They become part of our attitude. And information will be compared to norms established in ourselves; we learn to judge information on our actions, on our thinking. The basic norm is that of validity. The next one is that of reality (facts). In addition we develop social norms, religious norms, norms of discipline for ourselves, and so on and so forth.

Good-bad, pretty-ugly, true-false, legal-illegal, healthy-unhealthy—all are the semantic expressions of the comparisons made between schemata (sets) containing normative qualities and schemata appearing without the normative flavor. We may call the norms "imperative" schemata or "value" schemata.

The system of value (normative) schemata in an individual is changing, as the other schemata are also changing, but the changes are usually small. Seldom can we witness a complete and sudden adoption of new norms, one transforming the whole personality, as, for example, the "conversion of St. Paul." The total of imperative schemata and value schemata gives the moral attitude or character of a man.

In practical situations we generally act as we have acted in similar situations before. We imitate ourselves or somebody else. It seldom happens that an individual makes normative judgments because he became aware of conflicts between imperative schemata or systems of norms. The norms in an individual are more dominant if they are formulated, and judgments on the application of norms are consistent and reliable if the norms are known and not just felt by the person.

The Pyramids of Data and Understanding

We have to recall the pyramid of data discussed earlier in our book. The information available for the message is variable, depending on the decision of the provider of the message. On the base of the pyramid we have all the detailed data stored in the memory system; and as we proceed higher and higher in the pyramid, the data become more and more summarized (generalized). In this summarization process, some details are lost and others are maintained in a more general form. Finally, on the top of the pyramid we have only one judgment or statement left, a small group of data.

We can draw up another pyramid—this one situated upside down, resting with its peak on top of the data pyramid. It is the "pyramid of understanding," or the "pyramid of data processing."

This pyramid could be the picture of the data pyramid in a mirror, if by the use of the data the user would be able to reconstruct by interpretation and inferences all the data contained in the original data pyramid.

But that is never the case. The connecting links of the two pyramids are the data that are communicated and perceived. The comparatively narrow field of data is determined by the receiver by using certain clues in the interpretation process.

The interpreted data are already information. As information they contain more than as a sheer group of data. They are enriched by the receiver; they can be visualized as a much broader field. The information contained in the broader field can be interpreted immediately or in the future (unless it fades away), depending on clues acquired in the past and at any time in the future.

The interpretation adds qualities and broadens the field indefinitely, potentially to the limits of the total intellectual capacity of the receiver.

The shape of the receiver's pyramid of understanding is determined by the clues that he uses in interpreting the data and in making his inferences or by the schemata of concepts, impressions, and events in which his inner world is organized.

We may illustrate the correlation and structures of the two pyramids in Figures 8 and 9.

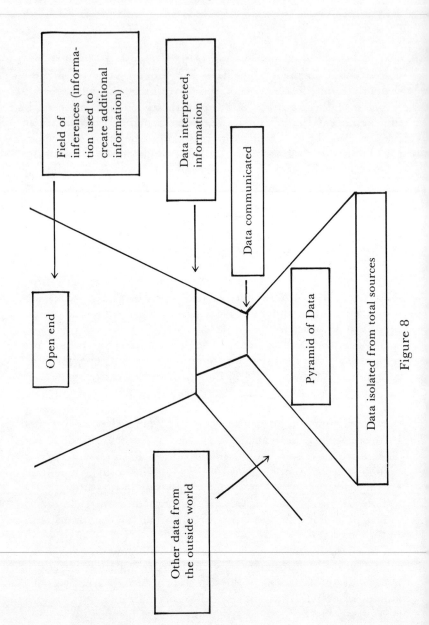

Field of inferences (information used to create additional information)

Data interpreted, information

Data communicated

Open end

Pyramid of Data

Data isolated from total sources

Other data from the outside world

Figure 8

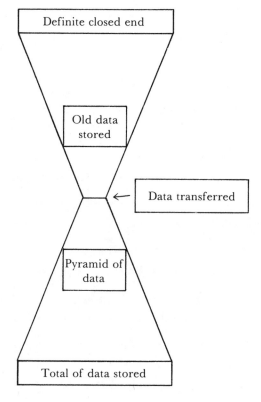

Figure 9

For comparative purposes we should have a look at the pyramid of data stored in a piece of electronic or mechanical data-storage and-display equipment and at data transmitted by it to another piece of equipment.

We can conclude by looking at the differences between the two diagrams. In both cases, data or groups of data were transmitted, and we assume that they were properly received. In the human pyramid of information, data are interpreted. In a mechanical device, they are accepted and immediately stored if the data are in the foim for which the machine was built and programmed.

The machine will reject the data only if they do not fit within the limits of its program.

The individual will interpret the data and will actively look into the surrounding circumstances for interpretation. His sensory organs are switched on as the result of data, and he follows after the receipt of data with an immediate survey of the circumstances (context). In effect, he never receives the data in isolation; he receives the whole world around himself, and the new data represent only changes in the world around him.

The mechanical data-storage device may store away the data received unchanged, or it may transform under their impact some of the old data stored and display them in a changed form (depending on the program), with the system of reactions built into the machinery.

The human mind will interpret the data according to certain clues and the prevailing schemata. It may transform the data into concepts or into visual or audio units of the memory. The group of data is enriched by the activity of the human mind.

The mechanical storage device will store the data indefinitely without changing them.

In the human memory the information undergoes continuous change under the impact of new data and information. It may be forgotten, transformed, and so forth. This "deficiency" of the human intellect—that it is a forward-looking and danger-warning instrument of the individual—is remedied by the use of data-storage equipment, be it an electronic computer or a pencil and paper system.

A young girl or fellow in love sees the whole world in a pink fog, reacting on data received differently, and all data end up in inferences and memories around the beloved one. Thank God, mechanical storage devices don't fall in love!

The human mind can make many inferences using the information created by the data as long as the human being or the information in his mind survives. Mechanical data-storage devices are not making inferences, but they can display or print the data stored in them as long as those data are not erased.

One of the main problems in human communication is to predict the effect of data on the receiver. How will he or she "react" if I tell him or her something? What shall I do to evoke certain information and action by the receiver?

If we have the opportunity to ask for audible or visible feedback, we can test the effect of the data under certain conditions. Repetition and drill have the effect of suppressing competing interpretation and inferences, and they create connections (clues) between sensory data and interpretation.

Further discussion of the problem would take us into the areas of learning, persuasion, and training, which are outside the scope of our present topic.

CHAPTER IV

OBSTACLES IN THE COMMUNICATION PROCESS

IF WE ANALYZE the relationship of the data pyramid and the information pyramid to each other, we can easily visualize the situations in which the communication process will not operate properly from the point of view of both parties involved. We will discuss the obstacles in the operation of the process.

DATA MAY NOT BE PERCEIVED

The first obstacle in the communication process is that the data may not be perceived at all by the receiver. There is no connection at all between the data pyramid and the information pyramid.

The receiver of the data in the communication process is a human creature. He is conditioned by his physical state: he may be tired, he needs sleep, he has emotions to cope with, he has an inner world, and he has many things to do. The world around him is full of data, which are competing for his attention. The individual's "data intake" ability is limited, but not just by the physiological limits of his sensory organs. In work situations the individual has to be sheltered from the onslaught of data that are foreign to his task. The presence, existence, or creation of data is a necessary condition for their reception, but it is not a guarantee of that reception.

If somebody wants to ensure that the data provided by him are received by the addressee, he must create a situation in which he receives the attention of his would-be receiver.

I recall the often-told story of the antiviolence animal trainer and Pedro's jackass. Pedro had a stubborn jackass which refused to do anything on command. He was proud of the healthy and strong beast and refused to hurt him, so he had to ask for the help of a trainer who claimed to obtain marvelous results without using a stick or a whip.

The expert accepted the assignment and arrived to start the instruction. He talked to the jackass, showed it carrots, and gave it carrots. The jackass was willing to eat the carrots but nothing more; he was not willing to budge.

Finally, the expert asked Pedro not for a whip or a stick but for a club. When he got the club, without any warning he hit the poor jackass on the head, so that it collapsed.

"But you are using a club; it is violence," screamed Pedro.

"It is neither a stick nor a whip, and I have to catch somehow his attention," answered the trainer. After receiving a bucketful of water on his head, the jackass slowly recovered and proved that he could listen to the commands.

If somebody is in the position to swing a club over the head of his audience, he may manage to create a climate that is favorable to the reception of the data originated by him.

DATA MAY BE PERCEIVED INCORRECTLY

It is possible for data to be received in a distorted form. When this happens, there is no connection between the original pyramid of data and the pyramid of information. The receiver is connected to an imaginary group of data.

Identical data or groups of data may be perceived differently by different persons or by the same persons under different conditions. Somebody may say "gun," and we may hear it as "gum."

A few days ago in Halifax I was looking desperately for a printing shop at 348 Young Street. I could not find the address. On checking again in the directory, I realized that the address was 34 B Young Street. In the directory the B was printed immediately following the number 34 without a comma or a space between the numbers and the letter B. Looking superficially and misled by the grouping of the data, I had perceived the B as an 8.

Books on perception are full of similar examples when the circumstances, the schemata, evoked by previous data or expectations distort the reception of the data. Those types of errors have to be expected if the receiver is tired or under stress, if he cannot pay full attention, or if the data are in the borderline areas of the receiver's field of reception.

The only way to eliminate those errors is to make an audit of the data, having as a purpose to establish that data were received in the correct form. The originator of the data can evoke evidence from the receiver by asking for feedback, for the recreation of the data.

The receiver may establish evidence by focusing again on the data, if they are available, or by asking for confirmation of the data by a witness, if a witness is available.

This audit is a form of the "basic audit." The problem is that the audit slows down the communication process, and we are usually short of time. In practical situations we apply it only in case of doubt or if the interest in the reception of the "proper" or "existing" data warrants the additional effort in time and energy.

DATA MAY BE INCORRECTLY INTERPRETED

Data are isolated, reduced from the total array of impulses received by an individual through his sensory organs. They do not exist in isolation. The individual separates or isolates them from all the stimuli or impulses received at the present and in the immediate past, while they are still alive in his memory. This isolation process—the recognition that a group of stimuli has significance and can be considered a unit—was expressed by me in discussing the intellectual threshold of an individual.

I was driving along a previously unknown road on a foggy day. The street lights were on, and I followed a truck. I could see a light similar to the street lights as part of the picture that I concentrated on in front of me. Suddenly the street light turned red. Only then did I realize that it was a traffic signal, turning from amber to red. I was not forewarned, not conditioned to see the light as data different from those of other lights. The data were received but were incorrectly interpreted, and I drew the wrong inferences from them. I considered the data in the wrong context. I did not receive data that gave me a clue in advance that I was nearing a traffic light. On long straight stretches, the change in lights, or a green or red light placed high over the road, is enough forewarning for a traffic light; but if the view is obstructed, as it was in my case by a truck, the amber light might just as easily be interpreted as another street light.

Actually it was a traffic light, and I should have interpreted the group of data as meaning a traffic light; I should have drawn the inference from its position that it might turn red, and then I would be expected to stop.

It is evident that the interpretation of the group of data is possible because we have a memory that is organized in schemata. If I have no idea about traffic lights, I will not recognize them as such. I may acquire "canned" or prearranged experience by learning about traffic lights. How can we avoid those types of mistakes in communications?

If we are users of the data, we need previous experience in similar situations. There are no two identical situations in our lives. If nothing else, the time of two situations that we experience is different; and if nothing else is changing in time, we are changing. Our inner world, the schemata and their interrelation in our intellect, is never the same, as additional information is added with time and some elements of information are forgotten or covered by dust.

Previous experience can be acquired by learning from stories, books, and organized courses. The hard fact about using these sources is that we face a problem: we have to transfer the learned experience to the actual situations. Try to teach somebody the intricacies of driving a car on a highway if he has never experienced the driving of a car! Books and lectures are useless if somebody has not previously acquired some direct experience in the field. If the gap between the experience and the data provided by instruction is too big, the learning by indirect data or by teaching material remains ineffective and useless. Eventually the "theoretical" book-learning may become effective if it is remembered at the time of direct experience. It may then "come alive" and help the individual in recognizing and interpreting the groups of data along the schemata established through remembering the learned models as parts of the surrounding world.

How do we audit the interpretation of data as groups of data?

Data never appear in isolation. Our sensory organs, with the help of our intelligence, provide us with a continuous flow of groups of data perceived from the world around us. Data, as such, do not exist in nature. We create them in our intellect, our inner world, by perceiving changes in the world around us and by cutting them to pieces, fitting them into categories of our concepts, and recognizing that data are in certain permanent relationship to each other. We make them by recognizing a "structure."

I am sitting in the room, and I hear crackling noises from the direction of the heating elements. I know that the heating elements are located at the window. I used to hear the noise when the heating was operating. I know that the thermostat is on, and I know that it is cool outside. My knowledge, the intellectual residue of past experience, gives me the answer: Without consciously doing it, I reconciled the data that were new in time with four or five situations, opinions, experienced facts, and my knowledge; and the interpretation fits in with the established previous experiences.

My mother's experience with the crackling noises was different. She was awake in a room, not her own usual one. She knew that she was awake, remembering the immediate past, by the feeling of continuity of sensations and by her conscious control over her attention. She heard crackling noises. She had no idea about the noises caused by hot-water heating, but similar noises in her apartment had indicated the presence of mice. Her clues, the similarity of noises, led her to the interpretation that the noises were caused by mice. Her interpretation led her to a simple inference: If noises were caused or originated by mice, mice had to be present.

What procedures could we undertake to audit the interpretations of the data?

a. We could ask somebody else who also heard the noises. Whether we could accept his interpretation is another question. If he is an expert, we would do so.

b. We could focus on the area where the noises came from by looking at it in the daytime when we can see. We could search for traces that are usually left by mice, such as excrement and openings in the walls; we could try to smell the typical scent left by mice.

We have in our memory a mental model of mice and the data accompanying their presence; we would try to find other points of contact between this model and the problem area. We would solicit additional data to extend our available data; and we would investigate by soliciting additional data.

In terms of the data pyramid, we would push deeper into the data pyramid and make available additional groups of data. We could broaden the base in the direction of the presence of mice and in the direction of the heating elements. If by adjusting the thermostat we could cause the heating to operate and make the sounds again, we could find additional evidence by laboratory experiment. In auditing terms, we would search for additional evidence by extending our procedures.

c. A third possibility would be to act on the inference that mice are present and wait for the results of our action to eliminate the cause of the data. My mother would set up mouse traps. I would switch off the motor of the heating system.

We would create new circumstances under which additional data would confirm or not confirm our inferences drawn from our interpretation of the data. The results would show the validity or falsehood of our inferences.

DATA CORRECTLY INTERPRETED MAY RESULT IN INCORRECT INFERENCES

In the process of the interpretation of data we can find all conceptual elements of a judgment or opinion:

a. The purpose of the interpretation is to establish the "reality," the significance of the data.
b. The norms applied are those of the "real world" as established in our memory by previous experience or learning.
c. The evidence consists of the group of data perceived.
d. The judgment itself is the comparison of the groups of data to our norms, our ideas about the "reality."

But in this judgment we are not in the position to change the evidence. We have to change the norms until we find a system of norms, a model of some aspects of the outside world as it exists in our memory. The resulting judgment or opinion will establish a relationship; it will give meaning to the data.

The inferences are the result of a second judgment, a second opinion:

a. The purpose of the second judgment is to establish the need for action or the need for changing our accepted schemata, our ideas in our inner world, our memory.

b. The norms applied are sets of our established schemata containing cause-effect types of convictions or opinions.

c. The evidence is the judgment, the opinion arrived at in the interpretation process.

d. The judgment consists of the synoptic view of the comparison of evidence, the result of interpretation process, and the sets of cause-effect relationships existing in our memory or imagination. The same evidence may be tied in with a series of schemata. In this type of judgment, a series of norms may fit the evidence. The application of different norm systems or different schemata produce different judgments, and all are correct. This peculiar conceptual structure just illustrates what we all know: that from the same group of data the observer may arrive at many inferences, all of which may be valid.

The selection of schemata as norms or criteria happens to go along certain "mental channels," the clues existing in our intellectual structure (attitude).

Perhaps we should mention that the concept of causality, the cause-effect relationship, is the inference in reverse. An effect may have many causes, and a cause may have many effects. I open the tap and the water runs. Did I cause the water to run; did the plumber, who installed the pipes; or did my wife, who paid the water bill? The causal relationship is a selective judgment. It is inference in reverse: I interpret the data received and then establish a relationship of the concepts. If the cause happens, the effect follows by necessity. But there are many conditions that are tacitly assumed in the validity of the relationship. Any of the conditions could be elevated to the role of a cause.

What does the word "wrong" mean in the sentence "The wrong inferences may be drawn from correctly interpreted data"?

From the point of view of the receiver of the data, it could mean (a) that he arrived at inferences that are false or (b) that he missed inferences that could serve him in promoting his goals, immediate or distant.

The establishment of the validity of an inference would serve as the purpose of an audit activity. Our norms applied are (a) the conceptual relationship between the data interpreted and (b) the inference or inferences drawn from them. The relationship is established by our experience in our memory.

The evidence is the inference, the judgment of inference itself.

In this peculiar type of audit we would extend the data base of the evidence. We could do it by (a) asking the opinion of an expert, (b) collecting more data about the event (the interpretation of the group of data), or (c) waiting for additional events, that is, extending the time-period of observation of the data.

But we could also check the norms applied—the conceptual relationship between the results of interpretation of data and the result of the inferences. Many inferences may be valid, and by reviewing an array of them we may find one or several that will serve our purpose, adding useful elements of information previously missed. This is the only way we could perhaps catch some inferences that we had overlooked.

There are no ways that we could determine in advance the inferences that had been missed. In retrospect, we may find the ones we overlooked. Therefore, experience, coupled with recognition of structural features (theory), is the best education for proper inferences. We may become conditioned by learning or education, but the learned "canned" and transmitted experience lacks the dynamic and lasting energy of direct exposure.

To develop the ability to make inferences is one of the tasks of professional training. During the formal educational process exposure to the cases of big blunders has to establish schemata and insight and make the developing professional man immune to the danger of uniform routine that is sometimes seen in professional practice.

THE CONTROL OF THE INFORMATION PROCESS

How can the originator of the data ascertain that the data are properly interpreted and that proper inferences are made?

The first condition is that the receiver shall be in the mental and physiological situation where he is capable of perceiving the data.

The second condition is that the message shall be in symbols or signs that are understandable by the receiver. If we have to communicate to somebody who does not understand our language, we have to use sign language or transform our symbols by using an interpreter.

In mutual communications, when the originator is able to evoke feedback, the problem is more or less solved. Naturally, a mere repetition of the data groups perceived by the receiver shows only the intended reception of the data, not the proper interpretation and inferences, that is, the proper "understanding."

To be able to understand data perceived, the person receiving them has to be able to interpret the data correctly and to draw the proper inferences. Therefore, the data have to be grouped adequately to allow interpretation and to be presented in the physical surroundings conducive to proper interpretation and inferences at the proper time.

Human persons are not machinery; they are not perceiving data in isolation, but they isolate the data from the surrounding world.

Another peculiarity of the human process of understanding is that inferences are made immediately on the interpretation of data. So there is a difficulty in controlling separately the interpretation of data and the inferences made from the interpreted data.

Therefore, in the control of understanding, it is futile to check the interpretation of data and the inferences from those data separately.

The following possibilities exist for facilitating the understanding by the receiver and subsequently ensuring the visible or perceivable inferences made:

a. Make preliminary arrangements.

Facilitate the understanding by the receiver of the data through proper training. If he is "programmed" to draw the demanded inferences, because he knows from previous experience what is expected from him, he will probably not "misunderstand" the data.

Put him in physical surroundings that are inducive to proper understanding. Uniforms and work environment are typical examples.

The receiver has to be "motivated" to understand properly by expecting that he will be rewarded, or at least not punished, for interpreting the data in the way that the originator of the data intended them.

b. Use signs, symbols, and words that are familiar to the receiver in the meaning familiar to him.

Symbols and words will be interpreted by the receiver. If he has to cope with the uncertainty or ignorance of the meaning, he may black out or misinterpret the data.

Every profession has its own technical symbols and expressions which an outsider would not understand. The potential receivers of a message have to be experienced with the symbols or words that they will receive. Even one uncertain sign can have as an effect the misinterpretation of the whole message.

Certain signs or symbols may have connotations. They may evoke certain clues in the mind of the receiver that may favor or hinder the desired interpretation and create competing inferences by him. Those words are parts of several preset schemata, some of which are emotional.

It is not enough to explain the intended meaning of a sign or word; the receiver has to be experienced in using the sign. Even a delay in the interpretation process may have as an effect the total breakdown of the communication process. A delay in interpretation may turn off the receiver's attention and prevent the reception of the rest of the data.

c. Supply an adequate quantity of data.

In discussing the audit of the interpretation of data and the inferences by the receiver, we mentioned as one of the ways to acquire additional evidence the possibility of pushing deeper into the data pyramid and extending the data base. The originator of the data can immediately provide more groups of data and thereby help the receiver in his understanding by furnishing more details, explanations, and instructions as clues for the receiver. It is almost a truism that the quantity of coherent data helps in the understanding of a message.

But data cannot be multiplied and extended infinitely. The ability of a human being to concentrate on data is not unlimited. Depending on the physiological and mental state, the motivation, and the memory of a receiver, there is an increasing capacity for proper understanding up to a certain limit. If the quantity of data and the details in a data group exceed a certain limit, which is different in every case, the capacity of the receiver to draw the proper inferences and to understand the data decreases. Mental fatigue, boredom, and inability to perceive the data, if

they are all presented concurrently, impair the receiver's capacity
to understand the data.

We may illustrate the process in Figure 10.

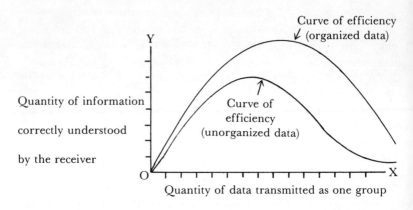

Figure 10

d. Organize data in appropriate groups.

Proper organization of voluminous data increases the receiver's
capacity to understand the message. Proper grouping helps in
evoking the clues for understanding. Data groups that require
either new inferences or a change in the established schemata
of the receiver should be introduced after connections have been
made with inferences that are already working in the memory
of the receiver.

In other words, if you want to say or teach something new,
you should start with something that the listener already knows.

The art of proper grouping of the data has received early
attention. The rhetors of classical Greece were teaching it, and
Cicero, in his *De oratore*, left for us what he knew about it. In
our times, courses in rhetoric, literature, creative writing, and
the science of education are dealing with the problem.

But we shall not forget that the organization and quantity of
data provided has to fit the situation and the expectations of
the person on the other end of the line. He has to perceive and
understand the underlying structure of the data presented. Otherwise the intended organization remains ineffective.

e. Discover misinterpretation of data and wrong inferences early (feedback).

If there is visual contact between the originator of the data and the receiver, the understanding of the data can be inferred from the expressions, the attitude, or the immediate answer of the receiver.

An observer can make inferences from data originated by the receiver of the messages. The expressions on the face, the movements of the eyes and limbs, and the position of the body provide an experienced person with ample data about the emotional state of the human receiver. The message may be interrupted, changed, repeated, or explained in the light of this type of direct feedback.

Every lecturer worthy of this name has to watch his audience for data (surrogates) showing the levels of attention and understanding of his audience. On the first signs of losing their attention, he has to modify his conduct of the lecture. He has to drop the main line of his message and throw in anecdotes and jokes to awaken a sleepy audience. He has to explain his statements by using examples, by repeating them in a different light. If direct feedback is impossible—as, for instance, on TV lectures—the originator of data is in a more difficult situation. In this case he has to lecture to an imaginary audience, and he has to do the impossible: anticipate the level of attention and the ability of understanding of the real audience.

The same difficulty arises in communication if there is no opportunity to obtain direct feedback. Typical of this situation are data provided in writing. If the organizational position of the sender of the message allows it, feedback has to be arranged in the form of recognition of the receipt of the data and in the form of reports, verbal or written, on the results of the action taken following the receipt of data. Proper action is the best proof of proper inferences.

If direct visual or verbal feedback is possible, the originator of the data can not only get information on some of the inferences made by the listener but can also determine the inferences that have been missed. The total array of data perceived by him contains more information about the receiver of the data than the contents of the original message.

In communications between persons who are physically distant from each other, as in the case of written communication and written feedback, the data received are isolated, and the sender usually gets back less information about the array of inferences made by the receiver. However, he is still in the position to find out the inferences that have been missed.

If no organized feedback is available, the originator of the data has to rely on his "image" of the receiver who will or may receive his message. He is lucky if he can test his message on a small group or on an individual.

CHAPTER V

THE ELEMENTS OF THE AUDIT STRUCTURE

IN CHAPTER I, we came to the conclusion that the postulate of communication is eventually not a postulate but a theorem of auditing. Could we not push deeper into the other postulates: the purpose, the norm, the judgment, and the evidence? Could we not consider them as theorems and find the roots of those concepts in some more elementary features of our human intellect?

Our further inquiry will render our preliminary terminology used in Chapter I somewhat illogical. I preferred to be illogical in my initial terminology, as I was afraid that the immediate use of the term "theorem" might create confusion in the mind of the reader. We used to hear about postulates but not about theorems. A relatively new approach to the audit concept, coupled with unfamiliar terminology, may run into "information blocks." It is better to be understood than to be precise.

But from now on I shall refrain from using the term "postulate" in connection with purpose, norm, judgment, and evidence. We shall call them theorems or, simply, concepts, and we will attempt to find the postulates underlying those concepts.

THE CONCEPT OF PURPOSE

Purpose is a relationship between the desired state of affairs and an act or instrument to move or change the actual state of affairs closer to the desired state. As the desired state of affairs is not the only one (we may have in our mind an unlimited number of them, some conflicting with each other, some not), the purpose is derived from judgment. In this judgment the norms used are the image or images of the desired state of affairs—the evidence, the image, or the model of the situation created by an anticipated action. The effect of the action as a cause is an imaginary one, an anticipated situation. The judgment is derived from the comparison of the anticipated evidence and the desired state of affairs used as norms.

Similar judgment structure is used in the decision-making or the selection between alternative types of judgments.

In previous discussion we illustrated the concept by giving some examples: the purpose of the audit of the crackling noises in my room was to establish the presence of mice; the purpose of the audit of the judgment of the judge was to enforce the law; the purpose of the audit of the applicability of a new production process in a chemical plant was feasibility.

What are the assumptions underlying the concept of purpose? Can we push deeper in our investigation and find the postulates underlying the theorem of purpose and make this postulate into a theorem by finding the conceptual framework for the concept of purpose?

If we consider the three examples discussed previously, we find that in all of them somebody wanted to achieve a desired state of affairs. My mother wished for a room free of mice. The judge wanted a state of affairs where law prevailed. The internal auditor wanted a situation in which he could measure the costs of a new process under factory conditions or explain the reasons why a process worked under laboratory conditions but not in the plant.

So, one of the postulates—that of purpose—is a desired state of affairs. This desired state of affairs exists in the imagination, in the structured memory of the individuals. The desired state of affairs may be something immediately achievable—for instance, to sit without my shoes on my feet—or something distant, such as happiness after death and immortal life for a religous person.

The second common element is an act (a judgment) or the lack of an act that will bring the desired situation closer.

My mother wants a room free of mice. The desired situation is a room free of mice. She has to make an audit to be sure that there are no mice in the room. The audit is an act that brings her closer to the desired situation; if there are mice in the room, she will set up traps and eliminate them.

Our assumptions in this case are: that human action geared to have effects does exist and that humans can foresee the effects of their actions. It means that we have here the element of human intelligence with the ability to foresee and plan the effects of the human action using the cause-effect link between actions and results.

In other terms, humans have imagination, and they can judge or have an opinion on the effects of their actions. We can find the following three elements in the above statement:

a. The element of human cognition (memory),
b. The element of judgment, and
c. The element of action. (We can act and, by our action, we change the environment.)

An organization or an object can also have a purpose. If we speak about the purposes of an organization, we use the concept in the same sense as that discussed above. The purpose of an organization or a business is to achieve or bring closer a situation that is desired by the person or persons directing or controlling the business.

The term *purpose* used in conjunction with lifeless objects has the same meaning as the word *function*. Function is a role in a more comprehensive unit. It assumes the satisfaction of a need for achieving the goal, the desired state of affairs, by the whole organization or unit.

The purpose of an evaluation process is not the process itself. The evaluation process is energy- and time-consuming. To be worthwhile it has to serve a decision, which has to be made in order to bring about a desirable situation or to avoid an undesirable future situation. The justification of the audit lies in the decision-making process. If, by concurrent or subsequent evaluation, the decision-making process can be more efficient or the outcome can be more reliable, the audit (evaluation) is justified.

To explore the interrelationships of the decision-making process and the audit, we have to describe and analyze the decision-making process.

The structure of decision-making and the audit. The report of the AAA Committee on "Accounting Theory, Construction and Verification" (The T. H. Williams Report, 1971) contains the interesting

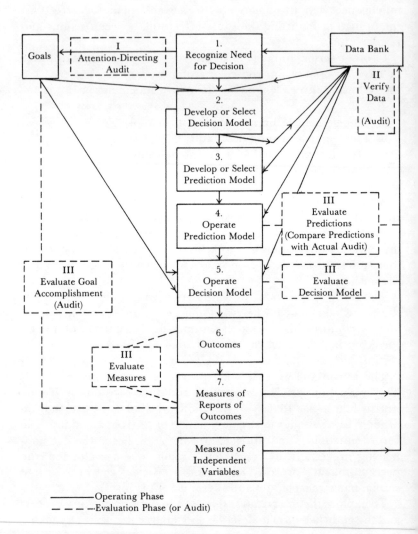

Figure 11

diagram found in Figure 11 (with slight modifications by me) showing the decision-making process.[1]

1. The first step in the decision-making process is to recognize the need for a decision. The need usually arises out of inferences made by an individual or individuals from data received previously. The inferences indicate a risk of not achieving a more desirable situation if an action is not undertaken.

My son tells me that his shoes are too tight and worn. I look at his feet (I evaluate his statement) and acknowledge his statement as true (valid). I need to make a decision: to buy or not to buy; when to buy; what type of shoes to buy, an expensive pair or a cheaper pair.

I have received a considerable amount of cash. I recognize the risk of losing income if I leave the cash in my bank account. I need to make a decision: to invest or not to invest; when to invest; what type of investment to make.

The next steps in a decision-making model are triggered by the initial step, the recognition of the need to make a decision.

We see that the need to make a decision is the function of two groups of variables (input): the goals that I have and the data bank (data available). The evaluation (audit) has its role in both directions: I may evaluate both my goals and the data available. If I use incorrect data, have no data about the needs, or am not aware of my goals, I will not recognize the need for a decision, and no decision will be made.

2. The next step is the development or selection of a decision model. The decision model contains the possible decisions that I can make. I can

a. Postpone buying shoes for my son,
b. Buy him an expensive pair of shoes, or
c. Buy him a cheaper pair.

Another dimension of the model is the method of implementing b and c. I can:

d. Go with him to the nearby department store, or

[1] "Accounting Theory, Construction and Verification" (The T. H. Williams Report), *Accounting Review*, Supplement (Sarasota, Fla., 1971), pp. 65–68.

e. Go with him to the Downtown Shopping Center and see the shoe stores there.

A third dimension is:

f. Do it after school today, or
g. Do it on Saturday morning.

As we see, the decision model is a complex system of different interrelated alternatives.

In the case of the investment of my cash, I may construct the following model:

a. Leave the cash in my checking account for future use.
b. Transfer it to a savings account to earn interest.
c. Invest it in short-term saving certificates.
d. Invest it in long-term saving certificates.
e. Invest it in bonds.
f. Invest it in shares of Company A.
g. Invest it in shares of Company B.
h. Use it as a down payment to buy a house.
i. Use it to buy a car for my wife.
j. Use it to buy new furniture.

As we can see, the development of different alternatives in the decision model is again the function of my goals and of the data available in my data bank. Again, we could evaluate the alternatives (audit the decision model) to make sure that all possible outcomes are there and that they represent my goals. In addition, I could evaluate (audit) the data used: are they reliable, "true" or "not true."

I may have as a possible decision the usage of my cash to buy a house or a car. But perhaps the house is sold, or perhaps my wife would prefer not to have a car for herself.

An important problem may arise in trying to set up the decision model. The problem is: Do I have the necessary tools to implement all the decisions? I may arrive at a decision only to find out at the moment of implementation that I have no cash available because I had suffered an unexpected financial setback. On the diagram we find a line between "Data Bank" and the "Decision Model." This line, as in effect all lines on the diagram, represents difficult and complex relationships which are oversimplified in the interest of clarity of presentation and emphasis on the "logical" structure of the decision-making process. The connections to the data bank, the validity of the individual decision alternatives and their exclusiveness, are of crucial importance. The importance may warrant an evaluation (audit) of the above-mentioned dangers.

By evaluating the inputs from both sides, I may eliminate errors from my model and thus improve the quality of my decisions.

3. and 4. After the "Decision Model" is set, we move it from the present into the uncertain future, and it becomes the "Prediction Model." The different possible outcomes of the decision model are projected into the near or further future, and we try to answer the question: What will be the expected situation if they are implemented?

The first question we have to face in this step is that of the length of time that we should use in our projection.

The next problem is that of the predictions of the future. To predict the future state of affairs is an extremely difficult and risky undertaking. We will discuss and analyze the planning process and its evaluation later in a separate chapter.

Assuming that the problems of how far ahead and what the situation will be are more or less arbitrarily solved, we face the third problem in the operation of the prediction model: How do we decide which of the future (expected) outcomes serves our goals the best?

It is easy to assume that our goals are best served by maximizing monetary gain or minimizing monetary costs. But how do we compare alternatives that are not expressed and are not measurable in monetary terms? How do we measure the benefit of investing in new furniture or buying a second car?

If the process of constructing and operating the models is difficult and uncertain, the evaluation of the construction and operation is even more difficult. What criteria or norm system do we apply in our evaluation process?

The prediction models are built on the decision model. If the decision model is multidimensional, the production model is equally multidimensional.

Let us develop our example with the shoes for my son. In my decision model, I had three dimensions:

a–c: Not buy; buy; what to buy.
d–e: Where to buy.
f–g: When to buy.

Our prediction model could be projected in the future, for example, to two weeks or three months: What will be the situation if I don't buy the shoes? Two weeks from now the present footwear will be totally unusable. He will suffer for two weeks. Three months from now it will be impossible to wear the shoes. I don't want him to suffer. The prediction model indicates a situation to be avoided. The feedback to my decision model (stage 5) of the decision-making process is negative.

5. Shall I buy expensive or less expensive shoes (b and c)? If I buy an expensive, good pair of shoes two weeks from now, the shoes will be good and my son will be content. Three months from today, the shoes will still be in good shape. On the other hand, I may run short of money for other needs of the family for the next few weeks.

If I buy cheaper shoes, they may be good two weeks from now, and I will have more money for other uses. But it is questionable whether the shoes will still be wearable three months from now. Which of the alternatives involves more risks and sacrifices?

The risks are: Will the shoes last? Will his feet grow so fast that the shoes will be unusable three months from now? What are the dangers of spending the extra cash for the better shoes?

We can come up with a judgment if we have a goal, a purpose, a system of norms or criteria determined by the goal. We simply compare the expected future situation (the future evidence) with the criteria, and the comparison (the synopsis) will result in the judgment. But what criteria shall we use if we want to serve several goals? How can we have multipurpose criteria or norm systems? My goals with the shoes of my son are conflicting: (1) I want him to have the best possible shoes, and I want him to have them immediately; (2) I want to safeguard my cash for future needs; (3) I want to spend the least amount of my time in buying the shoes; and (4) I want to satisfy his wishes, even if they may seem unreasonable.

The results of the projections will be judged against the criteria (norm systems) determined by the above-mentioned four goals.

The other dimensions of the decision model are:

d–e: Where to buy.
f–g: When to buy.

The prediction models are relatively simple. We anticipate finding the shoes of the required quality in certain stores, and nothing prevents us from visiting them at the time expected to suit both my son and me.

The evaluation of steps 3, 4, and 5 of the decision-making process can be useful. We are supposed to build our projections on information received from the data bank, our memory, and records. We assume that information based on past and stored data will be valid in the future. We plan the future and expect certain situations.

The evaluation (audit) of the future is complicated and difficult. We will deal with it later.

6. The last step in the actual decision-making is the determination of the outcome.

I decide for a cheaper pair of shoes because I want to stay within my monthly cash budget. However, after seeing the disappointment on the face of my son, I change my decision. I agree to buy the expensive pair of shoes that he wants. We decide to go to the store that carries the brand of shoes that he prefers, and we specify the time for the next day when we will go to buy the shoes.

7. Another step in decision-making is the action, labelled in the diagram "Measures of Reports of Outcomes."

The next day, according to plan, we went to buy the shoes. We were frustrated in a traffic jam, and the store that we intended to visit was closed. This was an unforeseen event, an "independent variable." The decision-making process may start again from scratch or from stage 6. However, our experience with an independent variable enriched our data bank, and we were able to make a more reliable prediction model for the implementation of the next decision.

After our explanation of the decision-making model, perhaps it will be useful to quote from "The Report of the AAA Committee on Accounting Theory, Construction and Verification" (1971) itself.

Relationship between Prediction and Decision Models

Research into predictive ability concerns itself with the issue, what are the parameters of the decision process and to what extent is accounting helpful in providing assessments of those parameters? Although this issue pervades all aspects of the decision process, the predictions that are probably most relevant are the following:

a. Predictions of future events or states (or probability distributions of them).

b. Predictions of alternative courses of action.

c. Predictions of outcomes or payoffs that will occur given the future event and the future action.

These three types of predictions are illustrated in the following table using several different decision models:

Illustrative Decision Model

	Investment Decision Model	Loan Decision Model	Linear Programming Product Mix Decision Model
Predictions of future events	Future price of shares Future Value of GHP	Firm failure or not failure	Cost and revenue coefficients
Prediction of alternative courses of action	List of possible investments	List of possible loans	List of products List of constraints
Prediction of outcomes	Rate of return	Losses or gains	Minimum cost or maximum profit under linear constraints

It is now necessary to talk in terms of prediction models as well as decision models . . . Since all decision models require prediction, models of some type are

required. The selection of both the decision model and
the prediction model(s) is to some extent limited by
the data available. At the same time the final model
selection dictates the kinds of information which must
be made available in the data bank.

The final operation of the decision model then requires goal specification, decision model specification,
predictions (least of the independent variables) from
the operation of the prediction model, and perhaps
(but not always) information directly from the data bank.
It can be argued of course that no data enters the decision
operation directly as data, but only as implicit predictors.

It is not always easy to distinguish a prediction model
from a decision model. For example, in the linear
programming product mix model, it is not clear whether
the model is designed to predict what mix will minimize
cost or maximize profit, or whether it is to decide the
mix that will be produced. In large part this difficulty
arises because in the final analysis decisions are made
in the mind of an individual. Even if the linear programming product mix model is built into the system, such
that the mix is automatically set by the results of the
model and it appears clear that the model is a decision
model, someone decided to allow the model to be a
decision. That decision was in turn based on confidence
in the predictive capacity of the linear programming
model.[2]

As decision-making is finally a judgment, by using the diagram
we can show the structure of the audit in the terms selected by
us as the theorems of the auditing or evaluation process.

The purpose, called "Goals" on the diagram (Step 1), determines
the development or selection of the Decision Model (Step 2). I
called the Decision Model System the *norms* or *criteria* to be applied.

The next step (3) is the development (selection) of the Prediction
Model. I called the Prediction Model simply *evidence*. Let us not
be confused by the future-oriented meaning of Prediction Model.

---

[2] *Ibid.*

The evidence can be anticipated or future evidence, and then it is a Prediction Model. But it also can be past, and then we could name it Historical Evidence Model. It could also be concurrent, simultaneously perceived, and so it would be a Concurrently Observed Evidence Model.

In effect, we can distinguish between anticipatory judgments, opinions, or decisions; concurrent judgments; and historical or past-oriented judgments. The structure of the three types of mental exercises is identical. Therefore, we could distinguish between anticipatory or future-oriented evaluations; concurrent or present-oriented evaluations; and historical or past-oriented evaluations.

At first, it may be surprising to hear about the "audit of the future," but we can stretch our concept of the audit or evaluation to include in it the future-oriented audit.

In operational auditing, in evaluating the effects of recommendations and in auditing budgets, we are dealing with "future, expected evidence." Let us not restrain the concept of the audit to the attest function.

The next block (4) in the diagram contains the words "Operate Prediction Model." This block refers to the adaptation of the evidence to fit the classes or categories in the norm system (as, for example, in a measurement type of judgment, the establishment of the evidence by applying a yardstick to the longer side of this table).

The next block (5) in the diagram, with the inscription "Operate Decision Model," refers to the judgment, or formation of the opinion, synopsis of the categories, and the pigeonholes in the norm system with the evidence model. Depending on the correlations, we may come up with evidence that fits in a certain defined category or pigeonhole, or we may not be able to fit the evidence into the given form and thus may not be able to arrive at a judgment or conclusion.

The block described as "Outcomes" (6) can be regarded both as the final judgment, opinion, or conclusion and as the reporting or communicating of the results at the end of the judgment process.

The diagram seems to imply that the action will follow the final conclusion or decision by following the "Outcomes" block with the next block on the line, "Measures of Reports of Outcomes." The effects of the action taken will flow back into the data bank but will be naturally mixed (or, rather, interfered) with by "Measures of Independent Variables," the last block on the diagram (which is not connected with the other ones). The "Independent Variables" description refers to events that were outside the scope of the future evidence, the "Prediction Model," by their nature or by the omission of the decision maker.

The diagram not only shows the analysis of the decision or judgment process, but it extends it by indicating the different types of evaluation or audit steps that are necessary to evaluate the success or the correctness of the decision-making or judgment process.

We can evaluate every statement, every judgment, or every representation. The possibility for an audit follows at every step of a decision, just as our shadows follow us. The data in the data bank can be evaluated or audited in order to establish their reliability. Goals can be audited; the need for a decision can be evaluated.

Therefore, the separate showing of relationships and activities that have to be evaluated is superfluous and even dangerous because by showing them we create the illusion that other areas of the decision-making process are not evaluated or audited.

But we have to analyze the purposes served by the multiple possible audits in the entire decision-making process.

I. We find that the immediate purpose of the audit may be to call the decision maker's attention to the recognition of the need to make a decision. We may call this type of audit the *attention-directing audit*. In our diagram we marked this type of evaluation with the symbol I. In actual practice the usual internal audit may be the closest to this type of audit; it results in a report calling for some decision and action to remedy and correct an undesirable situation. The external auditor's evaluation of the internal control of a client organization and his report to management may also be classified as an attention-directing audit.

II. The reliability of data in the data bank is very important for decision-making purposes. Evaluation of the data stored in the bank and, even more, the evaluation (verification) of the data used reduce the risk of making incorrect decisions. When the audit has as its purpose the establishment of the reliability of data in the bank, we may call it the *attest* (verification) *type of audit.* We marked the attest audit with the symbol II.

III. Finally, all the other evaluative activities in the decision-making process tend to ensure that the process itself will operate with the least possibility of errors or mistakes. We may call those type of audits *decision audits,* as they refer to the decision process itself, not to the goal or data used in the process. We used the symbol III to designate those audits at different stages of the process.

We may conclude that, according to its goal (purpose), we have:

   I. *Attention-directing audits,*
  II. *Attest audits,* and
 III. *Decision audits.*

THE CONCEPT OF NORM

What are the nature, content, and foundation of the concept of the norm? Could we find the logical foundations, the postulates, or axioms of the concept?

Historically the expression "norm" was derived from the name of a tool used by Roman masons. They had an instrument in the shape of a triangle with one direct (90°) angle, called a "norma," to obtain straight lines and perpendicular relationships in their buildings and projects. They used the instrument in planning masonry and stonework to develop "normal" shapes and relationships. So the norm helped them in their endeavors to create the desired forms and structures. It was something that they had to adhere to if they wanted to achieve the results of a desired quality. This meaning was later transferred to other segments of the human activity: norms of behavior; norms of conduct; norms of building, of beauty, of thinking (logic); and so forth.

We can easily see that norms, or systems of norms, do not exist in nature. They are the creation of human imagination as abstractions of certain qualities from the surrounding world, from experience. The norm does not exist in isolation. It exists only as a category or a concept to help the judgment—the classification between objects, processes, events, and results that are according to the norms (normal) and others that are not according to the norms (not normal). The norms are established or accepted as a result of a judgment: What shall be, or what are, the norms?

We may say that the concept of the norms makes a judgment possible; and without a preliminary judgment on the problem of what the norms will be, there is no judgment. It is a vicious circle.

The newly born infant has to learn the reality surrounding him. He will soon sense changes in the world by feeling pressures on his skin or changes in his visual, audio, and other worlds that are accessible by his sensory organs. As he matures and learns to move around in the world, he acquires experience about the data available to him. People around him use sounds, and he identifies some sounds with the visual groups of data that appear as a permanent set. He learns to use sound symbols to express groups of data, and he learns to identify the meaning of those sound symbols. He becomes familiar with the concepts as the abstract idea behind a symbol. Slowly he learns to differentiate between reality or truth and dreams, false signals, words and sentences that do not possess the quality of truth, his own fantasies.

Every child is a dreamer. This quality shows itself in his play. Slowly, between ages four and seven, a normal child can very well feel the difference between fantasy and reality.

What is the quality of the reality that distinguishes it from fantasy or dream? What is the fundamental difference?

We may find three differences:

1. If we are consciously awake, we feel a certain continuity. The data that we receive through our senses possess a certain echo effect. We can recall them in our memory even if they are not interpreted and understood. Sooner or later this echo effect fades away. But the interwoven perceptions create a sense of continuity. This sense of continuity, the schema of perceptions following each other in time, creates the feeling of present, the idea of conscious "now," the awareness of the existing and present world surrounding us with the feeling of aliveness.

Our perceptions while we are "alive," while we are "conscious," are different from the images, sounds, and events that are re-created in our memory during daydreaming or in our sleep. These last are "not in our senses," so we miss the echo effect. The differences are recognized very early in our lives, and a child is forced to make a judgment and discover the differences. The reality with its distinguishing features is established in the mind as a norm, as a group of schemata having "imperative" character. We learn those imperative schemata by a painful process. It takes years for a developing child to firmly establish the feeling of reality.

2. The second difference lies in the continuous and permanent nature of stimuli bombarding our senses from the surrounding reality. We have an extremely limited control over our sensory organs. We cannot help seeing and perceiving changes in our visual field of perception. We may close our eyes, but even then we cannot escape sounds, scents, and so forth. While concentrating on our inner world (our imagination), we may try to exclude the stimuli and prevent our eyes from seeing and our ears from hearing so that we can focus on our imagination. But this concentration requires an effort; we have to spend energy on it, and it results in fatigue. We are unable to maintain it for a longer period. In the play the stimuli of the outer world are not fully excluded, but we create stimuli to exclude the uncontrollable ones by using objects, figures, and processes to help ourselves in concentrating. The stimuli of the reality are everywhere and they break through; they annihilate the world created by the imagination. The permanent and always-present reality has a distinct and overwhelming energy. It is in our senses, and we cannot run away from it. This quality of intensity and existence is one of the features that helps to establish the strong feeling of reality as something different from objects, events, sights, and so forth, in our imagination.

3. The third difference is the result of the use of our memory for actions to achieve desired situations. In our memory or imagination, we anticipate the effects of some actions and nonactions as causes to create a desired situation. We can plan our actions. We can also act when we perceive danger signals, stimuli from the world around us which evoke reactions to avoid situations of danger. A child gets hurt if he is running and bumps against a wall, even if he imagines that there is a tunnel in the wall. If the child eats a make-believe dinner, he still remains hungry.

Action based on imagination, disregarding the cruel realities around us, results in pain, in catastrophe. The subsequent experience compels the individual to differentiate between imagination and the stimuli from the real world. The pain and frustration force the individual to recognize the quality of reality and to establish it as an "imperative schema," a norm against which the interpretation of groups of data and the inferences drawn have to be compared.

The ability to distinguish between schemata and to recognize some as imperative develops throughout the lifetime of the individual. A young person acquires the imperative schemata (his system of values) from the surrounding world—from his family, from his friends, and from social and national groups. Initially he adopts them simply by the desire to be accepted as a person who fits into the group. Conflicting schemata, conflicting norms, may evoke the necessity of making a judgment over the hierarchy of values.

We may conclude that the concept of norms presupposes the existence of the following postulates, or axioms:

    a. The postulate of human imagination (memory, cognition),
    b. The postulate of judgment (selection), and
    c. The postulate of satisfaction.

I could not find a better term than "satisfaction" to indicate the feeling inherent in human beings (felt by each of us) if we apply imperative schemata or norms in our judgments or opinions. The application of norms that we feel are incorrect or are not accepted by us creates a feeling of discomfort and unhappiness in us. The absence of this feeling, the inner shame, would result in humans without character, in humans with "moral insanity," just as the lack of ability to adhere to the "basic" norm, the actual physical reality, results in insanity, in self-destructive attitudes.

Perhaps it will be useful to survey the different types of norms usually existing within the memory of a human being without going into details:

1. *The basic norm.* The fundamental or basic norm is that of reality or existence. "I exist" because I remember myself, I feel, I perceive myself. The universe consists of the "existing world," which has objective characteristics and is perceivable by other human beings.

2. *The norms of Aristotelian logic.* (a) An object or a concept is identical with itself (A is A). This postulate of the Aristotelian logic is an abstraction, a norm. It disregards the effect of time

on objects. A is not A, if we deal with A in a different time. (b) Everything has a "cause" (causality). The causality is an extension (generalization) of the empirical phenomenon that we can change the environment by our action.

3. *The norms of physiological conduct.* I have to follow certain norms or rules in order to stay alive. I cannot cut myself voluntarily with a knife because I would be hurt. I have to eat in order to stay alive.

4. *The norms of social conduct.* I have to obey the rules of society as polarized in social and legal norms. If I do not know and follow those norms, I get into trouble. The norms of ethics, the rules of "good" and "bad," may be classified under Types 2 and 3.

5. *The norms of "taste"* (the rules of aesthetics). This classification is only an indication of the all-pervasive nature of the norms in the human life and behavior. All of it is based on the ability of the human being to compare schemata and to give more weight or importance to one schema over the other. This ability is the psychical foundation on which the phenomenon of "judgment" and, in consequence, human "attitude," "values," and "conduct" are built.

We may use the term "criteria" instead of the term "norm," and we may substitute "system of criteria" whenever we use "system of norms."

"Criteria" originates from the Greek verb "krinein," meaning "to judge." Criteria are the ideas according to which we make a judgment.

I prefer using the term "norms" instead of "criteria" because the latter term seems narrow for our discussion. It has the connotation of a past-oriented and definite judgment. Although it would still make sense, it would be strange to use the term "system of criteria" in a measurement or to speak about the "criteria of conduct."

THE CONCEPT OF JUDGMENT

We have to make hundreds of judgments every day. It is the most common mental process in our life. Perhaps this is the reason that for thousands of years the problem of the judgment has evaded the attention of philosophers and psychologists.

But do we make so many judgments every day? How many of our judgments or opinions are worthy of the name? Many of our judgments are mere imitations, slavish repetitions of judgments arrived at by somebody else whose statements, opinions, and judgments are simply taken over and imitated by us? Do we make a judgment when we seem to make one?

The grammatical forms for a judgment, an opinion, or a statement are identical: "The sky is blue"; "The trees are green"; "The water is cold."

The above statements represent judgments or opinions. The difference between judgment and opinion is a slight one. An opinion is less formal; it has no set and ponderous consequences such as those associated with the noun "judgment." The conceptual structure of the judgment, opinion, or statement is simple:

a. We have a purpose for each of them. The purpose may be just to communicate, to state the results of our perceptions. We want to write it down or express it, as in, for example, the statement "The sky is blue" (at a given place and time).

b. We select a set of norms (criteria) existing in our memory as a schema of colors, categories, qualities, and so forth. In our case with the sky, the norm that was applied consisted of categories or classes such as white, grey, blue, green, black, red, purple, silver, and so forth.

c. We select from the attributes of the object "sky" as it exists in our memory the one that corresponds to the norm. Our norms (criteria) used were the set of colors. The corresponding attribute is the color quality of the object sky. We match the color of the sky to the different classes of the norm, and we can fit it into the category of "blue."

The conclusion is the judgment or opinion as the result of the process of judgment, namely, "The sky is blue." We may communicate it as a "statement."

d. The judgment or opinion is the result of a simple process: It is a synopsis, a comparison of the norms and the evidence, resulting in an identification; but the norms have to possess a certain structure in order to enable us to make the comparison and identify the sky with "blue." We could visualize this structure as a set of pigeonholes, each one labeled with a different name.

The simplest norm is that of reality. Is it existing, valid, real; or is it not? This norm has only two pigeonholes: yes and no. We may add some more, if the purpose of the judgment would allow other results than a straight yes or no. We may add the additional categories of "perhaps," "probably yes," "probably no," or "I don't know," thereby qualifying or refusing the opinion.

If the purpose of the judgment is to determine the heat quality of the water, we use as norms the sequence of categories organized in a schema in our intelligence: freezing, cold, lukewarm, warm, hot, or burning hot.

The answers that the water is clean or that it is dirty would be incorrect ones, and they would indicate the erroneous application of another norm. By applying the required norm for our opinion, we determine also the type of evidence (attribute) to be matched against the norms. The categories in the norms can be compared or matched only against the attributes of the evidence that correspond to those categories.

I have to perceive the heat quality of the water on my skin or tongue and match the resulting impression (feeling) in my conscious intellect in order to allow the matching of my feeling to the appropriate pigeonhole in the norm. Without direct perception of the heat quality I may accept the sign stating "74° Fahrenheit" in the swimming pool as an indication of the heat quality of the water and say: "The water is warm." In this process I transformed the datum "74° F" into another form in order to produce evidence to fit the categories of the norm. If the norm's structure is such that the evidence has no attribute that can be matched to a category of the norm, the judgment is impossible. For example, let us use the norm of colors, as in the case of the sky. As evidence we select an action: my walk to the store. What was the color of my walk? My walk, as the concept of an action, has no color attribute. Matching is impossible and, therefore, no meaningful judgment can be made.

So the character of the norms and their structure (the extent and relationship of the categories or pigeonholes) determine the evidence needed to produce a meaningful judgment.

The best-regulated judgment is that of the trial judge or jury in a criminal case. The norms to be applied are the provisions of the Criminal Code. The Criminal Code defines the individual offenses in detail. If a human action fits the description of an offense in the Criminal Code or in some other legal statute, the act is a criminal action, and the person who committed the action is guilty of a criminal offense.

The pigeonholes, the categories of the norm, are the offenses defined in the code.

The evidence consists of groups of data from which the judge or the members of the jury reconstruct in their imagination a human action caused by the accused. In a court case the trier's position is relatively easy. He is not responsible for the investigation; the evidence is presented to him. He has only the duty to evaluate it, to audit it against reality, to verify it. So he has to make a preliminary judgment and establish the model of past events that he will use as evidence.

The evidence that the trier will establish is determined by the classes (categories) in the norm. The features of the model built from the representations by the witnesses and parties are the relevant features. Features of the past reality that are unimportant for the matching of the evidence and the categories (offenses) described in the Criminal Code are irrelevant. Nobody is interested in the relationship of a murder victim to his wife, unless this relationship could evoke inferences by the trier that would have an effect on the mental model that he builds himself from the testimonies presented to him.

We could attempt to reduce the judgment proper to the following postulates or axioms:

1. The postulate of human cognition (memory);

2. The postulate of synopsis (meaning the human ability of viewing concurrently two schemata as one system);

3. The postulate of selection (representing the ability to attach more importance to imperative schemata—norms—which remain constant in the judgment process); and

4. The postulate of identification (the ability to tie the evidence to a category in the norm system, which results in the assertion "It is.").

THE CONCEPT OF EVIDENCE

In the dictionary we find the following explanations for the term *evidence*: "1. The data on which a judgment or conclusion may be based, or by which proof or probability may be established

. . ." and "2. That which serves to indicate or suggest . . ."[3]

We may refine the terminology used by the dictionary. The judge or opinion maker is using information created from data perceived in the judgment process. The party seeking a judgment submits data or groups of data to the trier. Meaning 1 may be considered as evidence from the point of view of the seeker of the judgment who provides the data, while meaning 2 is evidence from the point of view of the judge, and the pronoun "that" should have been replaced by the term "information."

At the present we are interested in the concept of evidence used by the judge, which is meaning 2.

In the process of judgment, the norms are matched to the information that has been organized in proper form to enable the comparison or synopsis. The nature of classes, categories, or pigeonholes in the norm that is applied determines the attributes of the mental model made from previous information.

The judge has to structure or organize in his imagination, from information available to him at the moment of judgment, a mental model possessing the necessary quality of attributes predetermined by the norms to be applied. Evidence is the result of the reduction of information available to the judge. From the total array of information, he disregards the elements not having an influence on the selection between the pigeonholes in the structured norm. Information that would not result in different pigeonholes is called "irrelevant."

In the simple statement, "The sky is blue," the norm is a set of the different colors organized around the concept of "the sky." The concept of "the sky" was imposed as a governing aspect of the system of norms by the purpose of the judgment: to establish the "color quality" of the sky. We apply those norms because, for a purpose not known to us, there is a need for the judgment or opinion on the "color quality" of the sky.

We gather the evidence: We look out the window. We do not see the street below us or the walls, roofs, smoke, fire ladders, and other parts of the coherent and continuous picture emerging as the result of our visual perception. Our interpretation of the

---

[3] *The American Heritage Dictionary of the English Language*, ed. W. Morris (New York: American Heritage Publishing Co., 1969), s.v. "evidence."

data is geared by the schema of the norm to be applied; therefore, we focus on the sky, especially on the color quality of the sky. We organize the data perceived, and the information pyramid in us gets slanted so that we identify the quality of the sky with the color concept known by experience which is identical with the symbol "blue." As one of the components of the set of concepts representing the norm is the same concept (symbol), we can establish the identity and conclude that the sky is blue. But is the sky really blue? Is our statement or opinion, our judgment, correct?

It is true if (a) the evidence is true, (b) the interpretation of the data about the color attribute of the sky is correct, and (c) the inference drawn from the interpretation is correct. So there is an implied judgment on the truth or validity of the evidence in every judgment. And to ascertain the truth of the evidence, we need a preliminary judgment. The mental model of the evidence is compared or matched in this judgment to the basic norm of "truth," "validity" in our inner world, our imagination.

We called the evaluation of truth (validity) of a phenomenon (a group of data perceived or information created by their use) the *basic audit*. We may, therefore, call this preliminary judgment on the validity of the evidence the "basic judgment."

Unless the purpose of the judgment is to establish the truth, every judgment consists of two subsequent judgments: first, the establishment of the evidence, the acceptance of it as true or valid; and second, the primary or main judgment (opinion), using the evidence accepted in the secondary judgment as part of the procedure.

The establishment of the norm to be applied was another secondary judgment. Every judgment (or opinion) is a system of four connected judgments:

a. The judgment to establish the purpose;
b. The judgment on the norm to be applied;
c. The judgment on the validity of the evidence; and
d. The final judgment, referring back to the purpose and fulfilling its requirements.

In order to allow a judgment, the evidence has to be structured to fit the norm applied, and it has to be true (valid). The evidence may be untrue or invalid if somebody knowingly and willingly uses imaginary evidence or if somebody makes an error in the slanting of the pyramid of information available to him in his memory by making wrong inferences. The narrower the scope of the available information, the easier it is to make wrong inferences and to arrive at an incorrect model of evidence. The consequence will be an incorrect or untrue opinion.

The establishment of the properly structured and true (valid) evidence is the most difficult problem in every judgment. The auditor has the specific duty of establishing the proper structure and truth of the evidence by the audit procedures.

What are the postulates underlying the theorems of evidence? What are the basic assumptions allowing us to use the concept? We may attempt to list them:

1. The human memory (cognition). We can recall past perception in a form detached from the continuous flow of perceptions in time.
2. The ability to gear the elements (concepts) remembered in schemata, to organize and control our memory according to the requirements of the norm to be applied (abstraction and generalization).

THE MEASUREMENT

A special type of judgment, in which the final conclusion is expressed in figures, is called measurement. The analysis of measurement will help us gain further insight into the relationship of purpose, norms, evidence, and conclusion in the process of judgment or opinion.

S. S. Stevens, in his classic article, described four different types of measurement: (1) identity, (2) ordinal, (3) interval, and (4) ratio measurements.[4]

Identity measurement. Stevens called "identity measurement" the judgment in which a symbol of numbers is used in order to establish the identity of an object, process, or concept.

I am watching a hockey game on TV. I see numbers on the

---

[4] S. S. Stevens, "Measurement and Man," *Science* (February, 1958), pp. 383–89.

uniforms of the players. If I have a list of the players in white and in dark jerseys, I can identify the names of the individual players that I see on the screen.

The purpose of this type of judgment is to establish identity or nonidentity between two concepts. I see Number 9 on one of the players wearing a light jersey. I look it up on my list and, by looking at the name listed as "9" in the column of the team wearing the light jerseys, I can identify the player as Bobby Hull.

I used as my norm the two sets of numbers printed in the two columns, one set referring to the light jerseys and the other set referring to the dark jerseys. My system of norms consisted of these two sets, the light and dark. The categories, pigeonholes, consisted of the numbers and the names of the players as printed on the program that I had in front of me.

The evidence required is the number appearing on the jersey of the player. I see it. By comparing the number that I perceive in the pigeonholes in the norm, I arrive at the conclusion that Number 9 *is* Bobby Hull, and I see Bobby Hull on the screen. I may express my conclusion in the statement, "There *is* Bobby Hull."

Naturally the existence of numbers on the jerseys, the proper evidence geared to the pigeonholes in the norms, was a prerequisite for the judgment. As a connecting link instead of numbers, we could have used letters, signs, or even colors in the system of the norm and in the evidence. In effect, in our example we used not only numbers but colors—the light and dark jerseys were parts of the same norm system.

Is Stevens' "identity measurement" really a measurement? In *The American Heritage Dictionary of the English Language,* "measurement" is defined as "the act of measuring"; and from the many meanings of the verb "measure," we use here those that define it as "to ascertain the dimensions, quantity, or capacity of [something]" or "to estimate by evaluation or comparison."[5] The verb "measure" carries the connotation of numbers that allow comparison. In our example, the numbers were used as reference

[5] *American Heritage Dictionary,* s.vv. "measure," "measurement."

numbers, as signs to allow identification. The idea of "evaluation" or "comparison" was lacking.

We may conclude that Stevens' "identity measurement" is only "pseudo-measurement" and that the numbers in this type of measurement can be replaced by any other signs. These are not parts of a norm organized in a way to allow evaluation or quantification. They are not interdependent items, pigeonholes in the whole "set" of classes in the norm system, but are independent units.

Ordinal measurement. "Ordinal measurement" was the name given by Stevens to the judgment process having as its purpose the establishment of the order of items along a line representing a certain attribute of the items.

Let us assume that hockey teams would adopt the practice of numbering their players according to their weight. In this case, Number 1 would be the heaviest; Number 2, the second heaviest; and, say, Number 20, the lightest.

The purpose of this type of measurement is not the establishment of the players but the establishment of their rank within the set of players playing on one team according to their weight. The norm would consist of categories or pigeonholes placed one after the other on a line representing the sequence according to the attribute of weight.

To obtain the necessary evidence, we would have to compare the weights of the individual players. The results could be obtained without the use of a scale, simply by comparing the players to each other. Once a method is worked out to allow the evidence to fit the norm structure, the coach or manager of the team could assign the pigeonholes, the numbers. In this case, the numbers on the jerseys would represent the rank, the order of the players within their respective groups.

As a spectator I could see that the heaviest member of the light-jersey team is playing against the lightest member of the dark-jersey team, but I could not identify them unless the identity measurement were superimposed on the "ordinal" one and I possessed an up-to-date listing of the names and numbers of the players. If so, there would be an "ordinal measurement" by the coach or manager and, superimposed on it, a "nominal measurement" by me, the spectator.

I would know from looking at the numbers who is heavier or lighter in weight on the same team, but I would not know by how much or how little.

The difference between the identity and ordinal measurements lies in the structure of the norm applied. In the identity measurement the pigeonholes of the norm are unstructured, like a group of pebbles. In the ordinal norm the pigeonholes are laid out on a line: the first one represents the heaviest, the last one the lightest. The addition of a pigeonhole would push the whole series up or down.

Typical applications of the ordinal measurement are competitions or races. Twelve athletes are starting a one-mile race. The norms applied are the regulations of the race, coupled with the system of natural numbers from 1 to 12. The pigeonholes are predetermined, so that Number 1, who comes first, will be of a higher rank than Number 2; Number 2 higher than Number 3, and so forth. The evidence will be the sequence of the athletes as they pass the finish line. The first one crossing the line as seen by the officials will be Number 1; the next, Number 2; then Number 3; and so forth. The result will be the rank of the competitors at the finish line, an *ordinal* judgment on their relative performances.

As we mentioned, the basic difference between identity and ordinal measurement lies in the structure of the norms used. The classes or pigeonholes in the ordinal norm are interdependent, not independent from each other within the total set. The rank order is a quality of the structure of the set together with the specific conditions determining its nature and application.

In an ordinal measurement, the numbers could be replaced with letters (a, b, c, etc.), signs, or verbal expressions; but the letters, signs, and words have to be structured in a sequential rank order. The rank order has to be predetermined in a structure.

If the rank-order measurement results (conclusions) have to be communicated, the receiver of the conclusions has to know the structure of the norm used by the measurer. He has to be "programmed" for the proper interpretation of the conclusion or the judgment. Could we find a number in the telephone directory without knowing the alphabet? In the directory, the assignment of numbers to individuals is an identity type of gross measurement. The sequence, the rank of the individual names, is an ordinal measurement.

Interval measurement. In the "interval" type of measurement, the differences of one attribute of a conceptual unit from another (or from an imaginary one) are expressed in numbers.

If in a track race the time elapsed from the starting signal is determined for the competitors and is expressed in units of time, we achieve an interval measurement. The resulting numbers will allow us not only to express the time that each competitor needs to arrive at the finish line (one measurement of interval) but also to find the differences between their performances (second interval), expressed in numbers.

This type of measurement is the one considered to be the only type of measurement in the ordinary sense of the term. We can find it in almost every aspect of our lives. If we express the time as 8 P.M. or if we mention distances, weights, prices, temperatures, and so forth, we make use of interval-type measurements.

The difference between order and interval of measurements lies again in the structure of the norms that are applied in each case. The different norms will require different types of evidence.

The norm structure in the ordinal type of measurement is relatively simple. Here the pigeonholes, the classes or categories in the norm structure, are identified by a sign and are related to each other in a hierarchy. We could visualize the hierarchy as a sequence of the pigeonholes on a line:

START   END

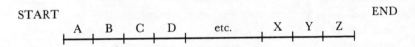

On this line, B is after A; C after B; D after C; and so forth; and Z is the last one.

The norm structure in the interval type of measurement could be visualized also as a sequence of pigeonholes, but the pigeonholes can remain empty. The quantity of empty pigeonholes from the starting point is expressed in a number which shows the distance of the attribute fitting into one of them from the zero (0) or other starting point in the system.

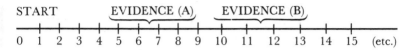

START   EVIDENCE (A)   EVIDENCE (B)

0 1 2 3 4 5 6 7 8 9 10 11 12 13 14 15 (etc.)

For Item A, the result of measurement is expressed in pigeonhole Number 7; for B, in Number 12.

The result tells us the location of A and B from the 0 point of the system and, in addition, the interval between A and B: $12 - 7 = 5$.

The pigeonholes in the structure of the norms can be multiplied ad infinitum to express the intervals more exactly and in more detail. We could cut the distance between 1 and 2 into 10, 100, 1,000, . . ., pigeonholes.

The system of natural numbers so commonly adopted by our civilization lends itself naturally as an organizing principle underlying the structure of the categories in the norm applied, but any artificial system in which the intervals could be expressed by signs having a certain relationship would fulfill the same function.

We shall not, however, commit the error of thinking that the norms consist of the system of natural numbers alone. Coupled with the system of natural numbers is the idea of units of time, length, or some other quality of the attribute to be measured. Without the unit of the quality, the system of natural numbers is an empty and unusable shell. In order to accomplish the measurement of a time period, we have to establish or accept the units of time around which the norm system is built with the help of the system of natural numbers. For measurement of weight, we have to determine the units of weight; for measurement of length, we have to agree on a unit of length.

Unless the evidence is expressed in the same units of time, length, weight, and so forth, we are unable to pursue our aim and arrive at an opinion. Evidence that is expressed in different types of units or that is not expressable in those units remains irrelevant, and the attribute remains unmeasurable.

The crucial step in every type of measurement is the establishment of suitable evidence. From the multitude of data available and from information processed in our memory, we have to construct the evidence in a form that is applicable or relevant to the pigeonholes in the norm system applied. We are developing this type and form of evidence by omitting the irrelevant attributes and by condensing the relevant data in our information pyramid (or data pyramid) to the extent determined by the norm system. If we are unable to perform the reduction of the data in the direction determined by the categories of the norm system, our attempt to measure remains futile.

In measuring the time that it took a competitor to cover a course, we have to establish the evidence in units of time—seconds and tenths of seconds. We need an instrument that can be set in operation at the sound of the starting signal. The mechanical indicator on the instrument, the watch, moves along a scale expressed in time units. The evidence required is the movement of the indicator. When we started the movement we excluded all other data available from the outside world. We had to forget about the color of the sky, the scenery around us, noises, and so forth. The only bit of data that we admitted to our attention was the sound of the starting signal. The indicator had to be stopped at the moment the first, second, and third competitors crossed the finish line.

The watch used in measuring the time is a tool that expresses the passing of time in units of distance by moving the indicator at a continuous speed. Humans do not possess sensory organs for perceiving the flow of time directly. They can perceive a sequence of data but not time differences. They have to express the flow of time in a way that is visible. So they use continuous movement at a constant speed as an instrument to provide both the norm system and the matching evidence.

The above example also serves to illustrate the necessary correspondence between the norm system and evidence: judgment is impossible if there is no evidence structured according to the norm system.

We want to know how many pebbles are lying on a beach that is two miles long. The norm is established: the total number of pebbles on the beach of two miles, expressed in units of the natural number system. To get the evidence we could spend our time counting pebbles. This is impossible; therefore, no judgment is possible. If we need an answer for our particular purpose, we have to modify our norm system. We could provide evidence about the number of pebbles on a small part, say, one yard of the beach. If we use the norm—one yard of beach, pebbles expressed in natural numbers—we can count the pebbles. By matching the evidence (the result of count—a result of direct, numerical series of perceptions remembered as one schema) with the norm system, we arrive at a judgment. By assuming that the density of pebbles on the entire beach is equal (an arbitrary inference) and by using the judgment on the one-yard stretch of the beach, we may infer that the number of pebbles on the entire beach is 3,520 times the number of the pebbles on one yard.

The measurement is made possible because we constructed an evidence; however, its quality depends on the validity, the "truth," of our inference about the density and distribution of the pebbles on the beach.

Ratio-scale measurement. The "ratio-scale measurement" of Stevens is a judgment that results in a combination of numbers, one of which is a numerator, the other the denominator, indicating a ratio. Professor Stevens classifies as "ratio measurement" all measurements in which the scale used as the structure of the norm applied is determined in units that represent parts, ratios of a comprehensive unit. For example, he considers the units of time (seconds, minutes, hours) as ratios of the 24-hour cycle, the length of time in which the earth makes a complete rotation around its axis.

The ratio-scale measurement is therefore a sequence of two measurements: the first, to establish the scale that will be used in the norm system for the second, final measurement.

Although we could explain the time units (hours, minutes, and so forth) as units derived from the rotation of our planet, their connection to the earth's rotation is absent from our minds when we use them. Therefore, I would rather classify the measurements with the help of the units of time as "interval-scale measurements."

In the real ratio-scale measurements, the measurer has to have the idea of the ratio within the scope of the measurement activity.

If the relationship of the scale (norm) used to the distant unit base is unimportant and forgotten, we have no right to talk about ratio measurement.

Typical ratio-scale measurements result in answers that are expressed in percentages. The preliminary (first) measurement consists of the determination of 1% of the previously defined object or objects. The next step is the final (second) measurement, using the natural numbers as pigeonholes in the norm system. By applying the 1% groups, or yardsticks, we are able to construct the desired evidence.

It is evident that we measure only an attribute of an event or object, isolating that attribute from the data surrounding it. We do not measure an object, for example, a table, but only its weight, length, and so forth. The same is true about every judgment or opinion. We never express an opinion on all features of a table; we judge its strength, beauty, and suitability for a certain purpose. We may come up with a multitude of individual opinions or measurements on different features of the table, where the central point for the "system of opinions" will be the concept of the specific table.

Unfortunately the limitations of time and energy usually prevent us from presenting our judgments and opinions in the proper context and in a form that would prevent misinterpretation and wrong inferences by the distant user of the data group.

As users of data that are presented to us as statements, opinions, and judgments made by others, we shall never forget that those statements were made for a certain purpose with the use of a norm system and a group of data as evidence. The judgment, or conclusion, is only the result, usually expressed in a short form. If we use the opinions or conclusions of others, we run the risk of misinterpreting them and of drawing the wrong inferences because we are not aware of the specific purposes of the original opinions and the attributes those forming the opinions had in mind when searching for their opinions.

THE PSYCHOLOGICAL PROCESS OF JUDGMENT

We may summarize from the preceding discussion the psychological process of forming an opinion or a judgment. As the measurer or trier, we have to perceive the norms as realities in our imagination. We perceive the sequence of natural numbers as a set, consisting of a sequence of concepts, each concept having a definite and determined difference from the neighboring ones in the system. Next we establish the evidence by selecting an attribute of the defined individual objects or concepts. In the measurement process we need a unit of measurement for this purpose. If the judgment that has to be made is not a simple measurement, we have to establish the evidence in our imagination as a structure of events or happenings, as a mental model.

Next we have to compare the mental model to the categories that are inherent in the norms to be applied. If there is complete correspondence between one of the categories of the norm and the mental model or image of the evidence, we establish the identity; we perceive the identity as such; and we conclude that the evidence fits the norms.

If the mental image of the evidence does not fit the image that we have about the category of the norm, we conclude that "it is not so" because the correspondence between this model of the norms and the model of the evidence is lacking. Depending on the norms, we may then seek other categories of the norms applied to see if there is correspondence or not. Or we may go back to the evidence and use additional corrections in our idea about the evidence in order to explore the areas creating the differences that prevented the positive relationship.

When is a judgment not valid? What is the psychological process leading to an invalid judgment? A judgment can be incorrect because (a) the norms applied are deficient, (b) the evidence is not true, or (c) the application of the norms to the underlying evidence is false.

We will deal with (b) in the discussion of the evidence. Now we are trying to explore the psychology of the false application of norms to the underlying evidence. The prerequisite of a valid judgment is the ability of the trier or judge to possess and to reproduce the mental image of the categories that are inherent in the norms. The whole set of norms to be applied has to be known, and competing sets of norms have to be excluded. It is very easy to write down the above statement, but it is extremely difficult to follow it in practice.

If we have a nicely organized set of norms—for instance, measurement of the temperature—our task is simple. But we have to make sure that the grades on our thermometer are in Fahrenheit grades and not in another system. We have to make sure that the evidence, the mercury position on the thermometer, is correct. The judgment is the reading of the grades determined by the position of the mercury in relation to the scale. When the norms are not so neatly organized, our task is more difficult. Different norms may compete in the imagination of the judge, who has to arrive at an opinion. Humans have emotions, a state of mind, and their mind's performance is dependent on many other factors. The same norms may provoke different mental images (models) in different individuals. The basic audit deals with the evaluation of data or information against the norms of reality or objectivity on the first level. Our image of reality is the result of past information. Every person has different mental schemata about the past. The individual's ability to acquire knowledge by experience is extremely limited. For our daily life we have to make decisions or judgments by accepting facts or events as true because we were told that they were or are true. We have no time and no opportunity to explore the universe as independent individuals. We are forced to accept other persons' statements and judgments as "objective" or "real," unless we are ready to die from lack of action. We formed our schemata by accepting information as true because we were told so. Additional data and information created by those data will be considered "true" or "objective" if they fit into our existing schemata labeled "real" or "objective." We have an established opinion about "real" or "objective," depending on our past experience acquired by learning, and we have a more or less vague feeling about reality.

The objectivity at the first level, the "reality," is the simplest of the norms, as it has developed within us through experience since our birth. With man-made norms the situation is more complex. We have to know the norms that are to be applied, but in most cases several sets of norms are competing for application. There are norms that I have to follow for survival, for success, and for the survival and success of those who are dear to me. We belong to social groups, we do not want to hurt those groups, and we are not independent of those groups.

The awareness of the norms is a difficult task in itself. Their interpretation is even more difficult. It is an exception to deal with norms that are laid out in neat and coherent categories that are applicable to all possible evidence.

The creation of mental images from the coherent categories composing the norms is an exceptional skill. Most people arrive at judgments or opinions by "feeling," by unstructured intuition; they are not even aware of the analytical structure of the judgment or decision process. The so-called experts usually imitate other experts who conveyed their experiences in literature or in direct contact with them, or they imitate their own thought processes, which they have exercised in similar situations in which they had success.

The human imagination is not an automatic instrument. The ideas about norms, the structure of norms, and the categories of norms are stored in the human memory in different, more or less coherent schemata. It may well happen that in the imagination of the judge the appropriate category will simply not come up because other schemata overshadow it. How often do we hear the statement "I did not think of it." We are living not only under constant pressure for more time but in the shade of our immediate emotions as well.

The coexistence of multiple norms in our memory and the lack of opportunity and training for a mental review of the norms are the sources of errors in judgments, in addition to the general lack of understanding of the judgment process.

The ability to perceive from our schemata a category of the norm to be applied for a certain purpose is a rare one. It requires the discipline of concentration. We have to exclude the disturbing schemata created by the permanent bombardment of irrelevant data. It requires concentration. Some persons are simply not able to concentrate. The concentration has to be elastic and manageable. The person who applies the same norms to every existing problem without considering the different norms that are applicable for different purposes is considered a maniac.

The skill to see or perceive the similarities and differences between the mental images of the categories of the norms and the models of evidence is again a rare one. The establishment of relationship between the two elements that are necessary for judgment is usually done without the awareness of the nature of the judgment process. It is generally a vague feeling, not an analytical and conscious process, not a pragmatic synopsis of categories of norms and models of evidence.

We may very well assert that people usually do not make judgments or arrive at opinions but instead "feel" them, according to their actual state of emotions, unless they repeat opinions or judgments made by others.

PRINCIPALS AND SURROGATES

To help us understand and analyze the structure of the evidence and the audit processes used in an audit situation when the norms applied for the conclusion (judgment) are those of the reality (truth), we shall start with the discussion of a simple situation and then follow with more complex structures of evidence.

1. (a) The sky was blue, (b) the sky is blue, and (c) the sky will be blue. In this example, (a) is a simple statement based on past evidence, (b) is a judgment based on present or contemporary evidence, and (c) is a statement or opinion based on a future evidence. The norm applied in all three cases is that of the truth, the reality.

The statement (judgment) that "the sky was blue" expresses a relationship between two concepts, sky and blue, by using a third concept, "is." This is presented as a group of data for the receiver, who has to interpret the data by adding important elements that are assumed to be known by the receiver: namely, the determinants "when" and "where." We have to assume that the sky was blue at a given time and place. Without those determinants, the statement would be meaningless, for the data alone make no sense. If the determinants are absent from the statement, they have to be derived from the circumstances.

We established quickly the requirement that the evidence has to be sharply delineated from the unorganized mass of potential data (stimuli) existing in the world around and in us if it is used for the evaluation of its truth or reality; otherwise no audit (evaluation) is possible.

Let us assume that from the circumstances (related data groups) we know that the statement refers to the sky in Halifax on July

20, 1971, at noon. We cannot reproduce the original events, the phenomena that emitted the stimuli resulting in the information underlying the judgment: "The sky was blue" on July 20, 1971, in Halifax. The time span described as July 20, 1971, noon, is gone and cannot be repeated. The past is gone forever; nothing can bring it back. It survives only in small fragments, scattered in the memories of humans who witnessed it. It is now organized in schemata and is altered through the interrelations of the schemata that made the survival possible. The "principal" has gone forever, but some "surrogates" might be available.

The past in itself leaves no traces, but past events may. Some of the events caused changes in the world around us, and we may be able to interpret those data and data groups and thus reconstruct a very narrow field of the past in our imaginations. Records may be available, produced by humans in a very summary way and for various purposes. Objects may be available and may be used as data to help in the reconstruction of certain past events. We have to interpret the data, and we may draw inferences from the information provided by the interpretation.

At this point in our investigation it will be useful to adopt the refinement in terminology that has been introduced by the semantic school of philosophy. In accounting literature, it was first mentioned by Professor Ijiri in his book *The Foundations of Accounting Measurement.* In distinguishing between the expressions "principals" and "surrogates," their meanings can be explained from the following quotation: "We call things or phenomena that are used to represent other things or phenomena *surrogates* and things or phenomena that are represented by surrogates *principals*." Professor Ijiri uses some examples to elucidate his terminology: "We use maps, because they represent sections of the earth's surface . . . train schedules are useful, providing they represent the actual arrival and departure time of the trains."[6]

In those examples the maps and the train schedules are the "surrogates"; the actual surface of the earth and the actual arrival and departure times of the trains are the "principals."

In other terms, "surrogates" are groups of data that facilitate

---

[6]Yuji Ijiri, *The Foundations of Accounting Measurement* (Englewood Cliffs, N. J.: Prentice-Hall, 1967), p. 4.

or suggest to the receiver of the data groups the development of certain ideas by inferences.

Whether given phenomena are principals or surrogates depends entirely upon whether we are interested in the phenomena per se or whether we are interested in the phenomena that are represented by the phenomena in question. The same phenomenon may be a principal for one person and a surrogate for another, or a principal at one point in time and a surrogate at another for use by the same person, or a principal for one use and a surrogate for another use by the same person at the same time.

Furthermore, there are not only surrogates of principals but also surrogates of surrogates, surrogates of surrogates of surrogates, and obviously various other levels. For example, the statement, "I heard someone say that today's newspaper shows a picture of the plant of the XYZ Company being flooded," which is a surrogate of a picture of the plant being flooded, which in turn is a surrogate of the actual plant being flooded. If we are primarily concerned with the plant, the plant being flooded is the principal and we rely upon the above original statement only insofar as we are confident that it represents this principal.

We use surrogates basically because we need 1) to discriminate principals and 2) to communicate the results of this discrimination to other persons (interpersonal communication) or to ourselves at a later time (intrapersonal communication by means of recording). If we are indifferent about discriminating principals there is no need for us to have principals represented by surrogates. For example, for those who are indifferent about discriminating various possible financial positions of a firm, the firm's balance sheet will have no significance. Similarly, for those who do not care about the right-of-way, stoplights are not of any use. On the other hand, if everybody can observe and understands principals by himself, there is no need for another person to translate them by using surrogates. Similarly, if the principals are expected to be available at any future time with no added costs, there is also no need to keep a record of the principals by means of surrogates. Therefore, surrogates that are used in our life are always easier to use in communicating with others and/or easier to keep for future reference than the principals which the surrogates represent.

Before we proceed further, it is important to recognize the fact that the products of an accounting system are always surrogates; they are useful only because they represent principals, i.e., the economic events of an entity. This point can never be overemphasized. Had the products of accounting systems been useful in themselves, as various consumer products are, the theory of accounting would have been entirely different.[7]

The Structure of the Data Pyramid

By using the concepts of "principal" and "surrogate" we may return again to the pyramid of data.

The foundation of the pyramid is a phenomenon, an event or groups of events, separated already from the unorganized multitude of total data that are perceivable by a specific decision to organize the data around an attribute.

For example, in accounting for a firm, the transactions in which the firm was a party are isolated from the unlimited masses of happenings at the same date and location.

Once the events pass the very narrow gap in time that is called "present," they are gone forever. They survive only in their surrogates.

For the person who is processing the documents (the primary surrogates) describing some features of the "primary principals" (the transactions), the documents become the principals. He classifies them, lists them, records some selected attributes, and prepares a secondary surrogate of the original transactions.

---

[7] *Ibid.*, pp. 4–6.

From the secondary surrogates, a third layer of surrogates is prepared, and so on. We may have ten to fifteen different layers of surrogates as we proceed toward the peak of the pyramid at always higher levels of generalizations.

Professor S. I. Hayakawa, in his book *Language in Thought and Action*, developed the concept of the Abstraction Ladder (originated by Alfred Korzybski):

The Process of Abstracting

The "object" of our experience, then, is not the "thing in itself," but *an interaction between our nervous systems (with all their imperfections) and something outside them.* Bessie [a cow] is unique——there is nothing else in the universe exactly like her in all respects. But we automatically *abstract* or select from the process-Bessie those features of hers in which she resembles other animals of like shape, functions, and habits, and we *classify* her as "cow."

When we say, then, that "Bessie is a cow," we are only noting the process-Bessie's resemblances to other "cows" and *ignoring differences.* What is more, we are leaping a huge chasm: from the dynamic process-Bessie, a whirl of electro-chemico-neural eventfulness, to a relatively static "idea," "concept," or *word,* "cow." In this connection, the reader is referred to the diagram entitled "The Abstraction Ladder," which he will find on page 110.

As the diagram illustrates, the "object" we see is an abstraction of the lowest level; but it is still an abstraction, since it leaves out characteristics of the process that is the real Bessie. The *word* "Bessie" (cow_1) is the lowest *verbal* level of abstraction, leaving out further characteristics—the differences between Bessie yesterday and Bessie today, between Bessie today and Bessie tomorrow—and selecting only the similarities. The word "cow" selects only the similarities between Bessie (cow_1), Daisy (cow_2), Rosie (cow_3), and so on, and therefore leaves out still more about Bessie. The word "livestock" selects or abstracts only the features that Bessie has in common with pigs, chickens, goats, and sheep. The term "farm asset" abstracts only the features Bessie has in common with barns, fences, livestock, furniture, generating plants, and tractors, and is therefore on a very high level of abstraction.

Our concern here with the process of abstracting may seem strange since the study of language is all too often restricted to matters of pronunciation, spelling, vocabulary, grammar, and sentence structure. The methods by which composition and oratory are taught in old-fashioned school systems seem to be largely responsible for this widespread notion that the way to study words is to concentrate one's attention exclusively on words.

But as we know from everyday experience, learning language is not simply a matter of learning words; it is a matter of correctly relating our words to the things and happenings for which they stand. We learn the language of baseball by playing or watching the game and *studying what goes on.* It is not enough for a child to learn to say "cookie" or "dog"; he must be able to use these words in their proper relationship to nonverbal cookies and nonverbal dogs before we can grant that he is learning the language. As Wendell Johnson has said, "The study of language begins properly with a study of what language is about."

Once we begin to concern ourselves with what language is about, we are at once thrown into a consideration of how the human nervous system works. When we call Beau (the Boston terrier), Pedro (the chihuahua), Snuffles (the English bulldog), and Shane (the Irish wolfhound)—creatures that differ greatly in size, shape, appearance, and behavior—by the same name, "dog," our nervous system has obviously gone to work *abstracting* what is common to them all, ignoring for the time being the differences among them.[8]

---

[8] S. I. Hayakawa, *Language in Thought and Action,* 3rd ed. (New York: Harcourt, Brace, Jovanovich, Inc., 1972), pp. 151–154.

ABSTRACTION LADDER
START READING FROM THE BOTTOM UP

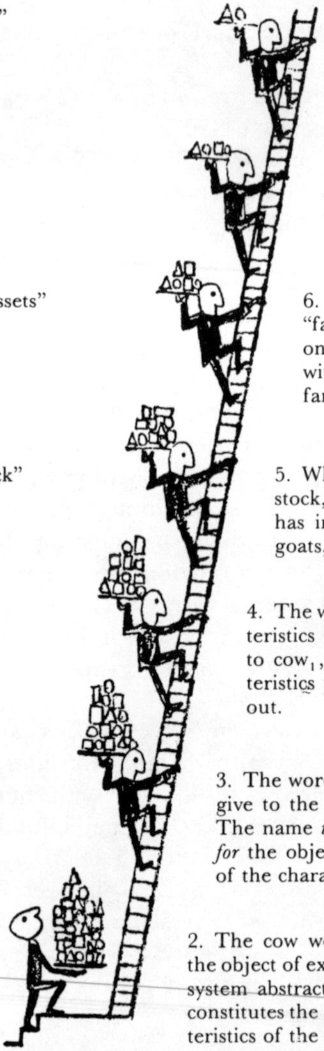

8. "wealth"

8. The word "wealth" is at an extremely high level of abstraction, omitting *almost* all reference to the characteristics of Bessie.

7. "asset"

7. When Bessie is referred to as an "asset," still more of her characteristics are left out.

6. "farm assets"

6. When Bessie is included among "farm assets," reference is made only to what she has in common with all other salable items on the farm.

5. "livestock"

5. When Bessie is referred to as "livestock," only those characteristics she has in common with pigs, chickens, goats, etc., are referred to.

4. "cow"

4. The word "cow" stands for the characteristics we have abstracted as common to cow_1, cow_2, cow_3 . . . cow_n. Characteristics peculiar to specific cows are left out.

3. "Bessie"

3. The word "Bessie" (cow_1) is the *name* we give to the object of perception of level 2. The name *is not* the object; it merely *stands for* the object and omits reference to many of the characteristics of the object.

2.

2. The cow we perceive is not the word, but the object of experience, that which our nervous system abstracts (selects) from the totality that constitutes the process-cow. Many of the characteristics of the process-cow are left out.

1. The cow known to science ultimately consists of atoms, electrons, etc., according to present-day scientific inference. Characteristics (represented by circles) are infinite at this level and everchanging. This is the *process level.*

Figure 12

From *Language and Thought in Action*, 2nd Edition, by S. I. Hayakawa, copyright 1941, 1949, © 1963, 1964, by Harcourt Brace Jovanovich, Inc., and reprinted with their permission.

It takes only one more step to develop the data pyramid from Hayakawa's Abstraction Ladder.

The ladder is illustrated as a slope. Now let us assume that our farmer owns not only Bessie the cow but also another cow (Bonnie), a tractor, some land, and a house which is subject to a mortgage.

At the level of extended human perception, each of those objects "known to science ultimately consists of atoms, electrons, etc., according to present-day scientific inference."[9]

At the level of our primary perception (the ground level of the abstraction ladder), we perceive our objects. Our nervous system selected those objects from the totality that constitutes the process-cow (Bonnie), the process-tractor, the process-land, and the process-house.

Each object could be placed at the starting level of an abstraction ladder. If we place the objects on the same level opposite each other on the perimeter of a circle, the five abstraction ladders will reach each other at the top and form the structure outlined in Figure 13.

If we cover the space between the abstraction ladders, we get a pyramid-like structure: the pyramid of data.

The pyramid itself is defined by the top, "Farmer A's wealth" (assuming that he owns only the five objects at the base level), and by the five objects at the base.

The second level of the abstraction ladders and their integration, the data pyramid, is the level of names: Bessie; Bonnie; Fordson, the tractor; Green Gables, the house; and Hollows, the land. Bessie, Bonnie, Fordson, Green Gables, and Hollows are already surrogates; the original objects are the principals.

On the next level to the top we arrive at the first level of generalizations. The surrogate "cow" stands for both Bessie and Bonnie. Here the individual edges ("abstraction ladders") of Bessie and Bonnie merge into one, and their individual differences disappear. In consequence, the data pyramid takes a different shape: the "Fordson" becomes tractor; the "Hollows," farmland; the "Green Gables," house.

As the data pyramid narrows and we get higher on the abstraction

---

[9] *Ibid.*, p. 153.

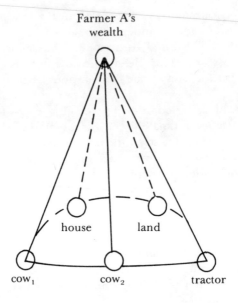

Figure 13

ladder, the cows are called "livestock"; the tractor, "machinery"; the land and house, "real estate." Here the ladders of land and house merge, affecting again the shape of the data pyramid.

"Livestock" is a surrogate for "cows," but it is also a surrogate for "Bessie" and "Bonnie." The surrogates at a certain level of the pyramid are representing all the surrogates underneath their special area and also the principals covered by the same area. The surrogate-principal relationship can be closer or more distant.

Level six of the abstraction ladder is the "asset" level. We have some trouble with our pyramid structure at this point. All the objects at the base—the two cows, the tractor, the land, and the house—are assets, so we reach the point where the ladders come together and form the peak. We get a very irregular pyramid because we started at the bottom with our five objects and omitted the "negative" asset, the mortgage.

We may say that the concept "house" has been split into the "house" and the "mortgage," and we could regard the resulting form as an edge. And this edge is transformed into a peak, forming the top on the level of "wealth," the highest level of the abstraction ladders.

In developing and explaining the abstraction ladder, Professor Hayakawa gave the instructions: "start reading from the bottom UP." For the purposes of determining the territory to be covered by auditing procedures, we have to consider the data pyramid as a volume determined by the top or by an area at a certain level.

If the audit calls for the verification of the wealth of Farmer Smith, we have to draw up the "audit territory," or "audit volume." In our imagination from our previous knowledge, we possess a model of "wealth." "Wealth" (material wealth at a certain moment) consists of assets less liabilities. Going down from the asset-liability level, we have farm assets, personal assets, and business assets. Liabilities are split into farm liabilities, personal liabilities, and other business liabilities.

Each of the above components of the data pyramid at one level can be subdivided at a lower level. The farm assets are livestock, machinery, land, farm, and stocks of hay, seed, and grain.

For determining the audit area (the audit territory), we have to include all potentially existing classes of farm assets, as in our inquiry we have to get an answer to the question, What are all the farm assets owned by Farmer Smith?

Disregarding the other concepts for our illustration, we will concentrate on the "livestock." Livestock may include cows, heifers, horses, pigs, and poultry. Our audit territory has to include all the possible types of livestock.

By descending to the level of "cow," we are required to inquire about Bessie, Bonnie, and any other cow.

We may end up by inspecting Bonnie and Bessie in order to gather direct evidence about their existence and by inquiring whether any other cow is owned by Farmer Smith or not. If we see a third cow with Bessie and Bonnie, we will look for evidence that the cow does not belong to Farmer Smith.

If we proceed from the top to the bottom down to the "primary principal" level of the pyramid, we will get a structure that is pyramid-shaped, with more and more details as we approach the base level (the perception level).

CHAPTER VI
THE PROCEDURES

AUDIT PROCEDURES, in the broadest meaning of the term, include all the procedures connected with the audit process itself. They may be performed by the auditor or by anybody who is setting the purpose (goal) of the audit, who is setting the norms or pointing out the purported evidence, or who is contributing evidence for the auditor.

The noun "procedure" has the following meanings according to *The American Heritage Dictionary of the English Language:* "1. A manner of proceeding, way of performing or effecting something; 2. An act, composed of steps, course of action; 3. A set of established forms or methods for conducting the affairs of a business, legislative body or court of law."[1]

For our present discussion using meaning 1 of the term "procedure," we will inquire into the "manner of proceeding," into the way of performing an audit.

Every audit is organized around the purpose or goal of the audit. The purpose is the guiding star of all the following procedures. It defines the norms to be applied and the evidence to be determined.

The audit in isolation (audit for the sake of audit) does not exist. In itself it is a mere instrument to help in decisions or to provide information for potential decision-making in the future.

An individual may decide to audit for verification purposes if the information arrived at from data or groups of data is of some importance. He will probably do so if a problem (or an expected problem) situation warrants the effort and time needed for the verification (basic audit) process.

Everybody is familiar with the neurotic person who is never

---

[1] *The American Heritage Dictionary of the English Language*, ed. W. Morris (New York: American Heritage Publishing Co., 1969), s.v. "procedure."

sure of the information stored in his memory and has no time for decisions and actions because he has to audit or verify everything.

How often do we check our plane ticket before boarding a plane? And how often do we have to search for it again when we have to present it at the counter? The audit syndrome in an individual can create severe problems.

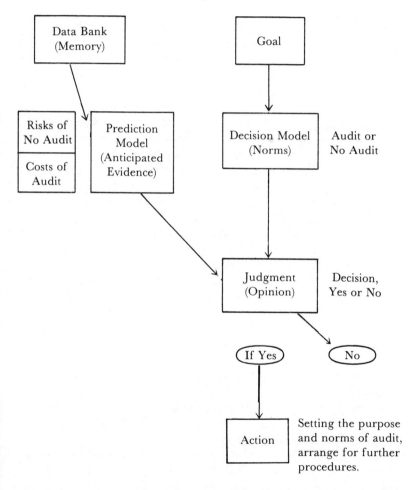

Figure 14

Actually the judgment of whether to audit (verify) or not is the most important step in the audit process. Not to audit is a risk that we have to take very often in our lives. We may illustrate the decision (judgment) to audit or not to audit in Figure 14.

SELECTION OF THE NORMS

In an *attention-directing audit* the goal is to call the decision maker's attention to a situation that may or may not endanger the achievement of a desired situation. Remedial action could follow, or it could be unnecessary. The first set of norms (criteria) in this case is that of the "reality." What did actually happen, what is the "truth"? Once the "truth" is established, the "true" situation has to be matched to the norm system, satisfying the desires of the decision maker. If the decision maker (the user of the auditor's report) considers a desired situation "adherence to the operating manual," the norm system is set by the terms of the operating manual and the terms of the final opinion: (a) complete adherence, (b) adherence with exception, or (c) no adherence.

In the *attest audit* the decision maker may use the information as input for a decision. This type of audit is restricted to the phase of "verification," the establishment of the "truth" expressed at the level of generalizations required for the decision. The "reality" or "truth" of some attributes does not exist and has never existed above the sensory level of our perception. When it is communicated it becomes a system of surrogates. The auditor has to use a system of norms organized in categories that are understandable and usable by the decision maker. The auditor's opinion cannot defeat the purpose of the audit by its details and its length.

In the *decision audit* the norm system consists of a "better" decision. The audit itself follows step by step the original or proposed decision through the different stages of the decision-making process. The auditor has to establish or verify the actual or proposed decision. The first system of norms used is again that of the "reality." Next he has to use the criteria (norms) of "truth" or "reality," again to verify the input from the data bank (available information). In the following stage the actual or proposed decision model is matched against a more complete (better, according to the auditor's judgment) decision model. The same procedure is applied to the different prediction models.

We can find decision audits usually in the field of operational audits and anticipatory audits (as in the audit of a budget).

In a verification (attest audit) situation the purpose of the audit is to establish "truth." Therefore, the norm structure is polarized into two categories—"true" and "not true." In the actual past or present there is not such thing as "absolute 100% foolproof" truth in the philosophical sense of the concept "true" or "real." We obtain our ideas through our senses from data groups that have been perceived or interpreted and through inferences. They are stored in our memory, and we cannot exclude the possibility of errors occurring in perception, interpretation, inferences, and memory. But we are unable to plan and act without accepting the hypothesis of "truth" or "reality."

If the purpose of the audit allows for such judgments as "true," "probably true," "probably not true," and "I don't know," we have a norm model of different structures with five tails instead of the previous two-tailed structure. We may try to illustrate the foregoing by drawing up the following map of the norm model for a true–not true situation:

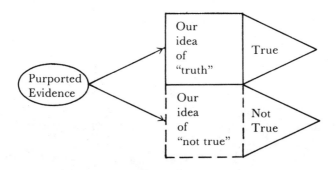

Figure 15

The five-tailed norm system, which allows for the additional "probably true," "probably not true," and "I don't know" judgments, could be illustrated as follows:

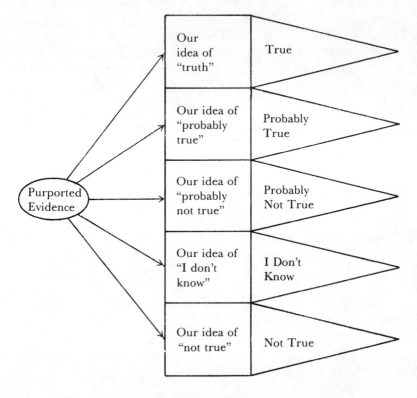

Figure 16

The illustrations show both sides of the norm structure: the "outcome" side (with the tails) and the "input" side (with the classes or pigeonholes) to accommodate the properly organized features or attributes of the evidence.

It is easy to analyze and describe the form of the norm model and to discuss its place in the audit process, but it is difficult to find a way to outline the relationship of the content of the norm model to the goal (purpose) of the audit. The purpose of an audit may be to provide additional information for actual or potential decision-making and for the action implementing the decision (attention-directing).

Our task will be easier if we review our examples mentioned in Chapter I: the cases of the mice (1), of the judge (2), and of the chemical plant (3).

In case 1 the audit served a potential decision to eliminate the mice; the goal of the potential decision-making was a house without mice. The norm system selected for the audit was truth or reality. The crucial attribute in the situation was the presence of mice.

The "purported evidence" (mice are there because mice caused the noise) was a surrogate of the principal—that mice were in the room. Surrogate A (representation) was tested under close observation (visual observance of the cat) and was found to be invalid or not true because the behavior of the cat (Surrogate B) did not conform to the behavior of a cat when smelling mice. The purpose of the audit was to attest a representation in order to eliminate needless decisions and action.

In case 2 the goal of the judge was to enforce the law. In effect, case 2 is not a clear-cut audit. It is closer to a decision-making process. The audit process is the establishment of the evidence by the judge, who hears the purported evidence presented by the prosecutor (Surrogate A) and other surrogates until he is able to establish the truth (the evidence model). His audit procedures result in his first subjudgment: "Those are the facts as established by the court" (attest audit). The norms applied are again those of the truth or reality. He will use the "true" evidence for the second phase of his activity after adjusting it to fit the categories specified by the Criminal Code.

In case 3 the goal of the potential decision-making was to save costs by introducing a new process. The purpose of the operational audit was to establish feasibility (future reality under plant conditions). The norms applied were "future reality" and "future truth" (decision).

As the auditor was unable to test the evidence step by step to the norms (operations under plant conditions), he had to recreate the plant machinery so as to fit laboratory conditions. The norm system was truth (reality) and the crucial attribute was the feasibility of a new process. In essence the evaluation process was preceded by an investigation, an activity to build up evidence.

We may conclude with the general statement that the first system of norms used in every audit process is the norm of reality or truth (verification).

There are audit purposes (goals) that require the application of another norm system and another opinion (judgment) after the truth (reality) of the evidence is established. We mentioned earlier the audit by the shareholders' auditor (statutory audit), and we outlined its structure in Figure 3. Here the auditor had to establish first that the statements presented the truth, and then he had to see that the truth was presented in the form required by statutes and regulations.

If the purpose of an operational audit is not only to establish the truth or validity of the reports (accounting and other) of a department but also to make recommendations to improve the operations, we face a similar audit structure. The first duty of the operational auditor is to match the purported evidence (records, reports) against the primary norm (criteria) of truth. Next he has to proceed and compare the true operations to the norms of improved or more efficient operations and then give an opinion on the efficiency of the existing way of operations. He may start his audit without even having an idea about the more efficient way of operations. He will create his norm model of "more efficient" as he inquires into the existing operations. His experience in the field and his knowledge of actual operations enable him to draw up in his imagination methods that are more efficient or better than the actual ones as he perceived them. After his primary judgment establishing the truth, he will match the truth to a norm (the better or more efficient operations, as they are generated in his imagination) by inquiring into and observing the existing procedures.

In our well-discussed example of operational audit (the feasibility of a new process working under lab conditions but not in the plant), which is outlined and illustrated in Figure 6, the situation was similar: the auditor had to create new norms (operations of equipment reduced to manageable and observable size) in order to form an opinion.

In example 2 (the judge's judgment) the decision was also a

sequence of two judgments: first, the establishment of the evidence; and next, the matching of the true evidence against the norm system, in this case the provisions of the Criminal Code.

The second set of norms to be applied in the above-mentioned two-phase audits (truth and another system of norms) follows directly from the purpose of the audit. We can derive them directly from the purpose if the purpose is specified verbally or in writing.

The question may arise in conjunction with the two-phase audit processes: Are those processes audits or not? Did we perhaps stretch the concept of audit too far by including in it the second-phase judgments? Is the audit of the shareholders' auditor in a corporation not finished once the auditor has established the evidence? Actually the second-phase activity—the comparison of the truth or reality to the financial statements to be published—is a sheer comparison, an evaluation, a judgment without further inquiry. Did the audit process itself not end after the truth of the evidence was established?

In example 1 (the mice) the purpose of the audit was to examine the truth of the purported evidence. Is the proposition "Mice are in the room because their noises can be heard" true or not true? In this case the audit was a single-phase audit, and no second judgment followed the first one; this established as truth that there were no mice in the room. The findings were needed for a decision-making process, and the audit process came to an end.

In case 3 (the new chemical process) we find again two judgments. The first phase is the judgment on the purported evidence: The new process works under lab conditions. The second phase: Compare the evidence to the newly created norms, namely, the plant-equipment model reduced to fit lab conditions.

Was the second step an audit? Is it not a simple "evaluation," a comparison?

The situation is the same in case 2 (the judgment in a criminal case). The establishment of the evidence by the judge from eventually conflicting representations of the prosecution, defense, and witnesses may be called an audit. But can we consider the final judgment of the court part of the audit process?

We may very well restrict our view on auditing and consider as audit only the evaluation of purported evidence against the reality or truth. And we would be justified to take the narrower view on the audit concept by giving other names to the second judgment phase in the process.

We could call the second judgment "evaluation" or "conclusion," terms having broader meaning than the term "audit."

There are three reasons for adopting the broader, all-inclusive meaning for audit and audit processes.

The first reason is that the form of the evidence, the attributes along which the evidence has to be established, are not irrelevant. They depend on the norm-structure requirements set up by the second and final judgment. The shareholders' auditor has to arrive at the truth of the financial statements as they will be presented. It would be misleading to break down an activity into subsystems because we may lose sight of their interdependence and of the wholeness of the audit process.

The second reason is the similarity between the two phases. The auditor has to arrive at an opinion (judgment) on the truth of the purported evidence. In this phase of the audit he is using the norm system of "reality" for his judgment. The second-phase judgment is a very similar procedure, using a new system of norms.

The third reason is very pragmatic. The same persons are involved in both, or perhaps more, phases of the audit and the final opinion. Our inquiry into the audit activity would be incomplete if we were not to consider the later phases of the activity and were to restrict it to the first (evidential inquiry and judgment) phase alone.

VERIFICATION OF THE EVIDENCE

Sometimes we use the expression "audit procedures" in the narrower sense of the words. In this sense "audit procedures" describe the procedures of inquiry resulting in an opinion on the purported evidence. We will use the expression "audit inquiry," or inquiry, to represent the diverse activities having as their purpose the production of data for the auditor about the reality of the purported evidence.

The 1972 Committee Report of the AAA (ASOBAC) uses the expression "investigation" to describe the auditor's procedures that are directed towards the establishment of the truth of the purported evidence.

"Investigation" is a term already used by the legal profession, by the police, and by accountants. It is used to represent procedures having as their goal the establishment of missing evidence from traces (surrogates) left by an event. We have to distinguish between audit and investigations. In the audit process we are dealing with purported evidence. In the investigation process we have no evidence, and our procedures are geared to the creation or restoration of the evidence. We can audit after an investigation has presented us with purported evidence. The distinction between investigation and inquiry seems to be only a semantic one. For the sake of clarity I will not use the term "investigation" as part of the audit process, as by using the expression "inquiry" we can avoid misinterpretation and confusion.

The purported evidence consists of one or a group of representations, or surrogates. These surrogates supposedly represent an isolated group of events or objects organized into a unit. Such a unit determines the ultimate principal in a data pyramid. Between the ultimate principal and the surrogates perceived as a group of data by the auditor, we may have several layers of intermediate surrogates.

The auditor is only a human being. His scope of memory, his knowledge, and his intelligence are limited. In his judgment about the truth, he has to match, in a synopsis, the surrogates presented with the norm system (criteria) of truth. Ideally, that would require a synopsis of the group of surrogates (purported evidence) and the ultimate principal (the truth as it happened and when it happened).

Unfortunately, the surrogates and the ultimate principal are usually too far from each other to allow a simple synopsis.

An auditor in classical Rome was an officer of the state or city who was present when an event (a transaction) took place. He did not participate actively but just observed and listened ("audio" means "I listen," "I hear"). The auditor was the man who heard the events, who listened to the transactions. His duty was to observe the events and to report if something was incorrectly represented or if funds were not used in the prescribed manner. His presence meant a direct access to the ultimate principal, the

individual transactions performed within his immediate scope of
observation. His audit was a direct and concurrent audit. By relying
on his sensory organs, he was able to remember if something
were true or not. He knew the framework, the set of norms,
the regulations directing the acting officers of the state. He had
no doubt about the events and transactions negotiated in front
of him. The ultimate principal was within his reach. This situation,
the "concurrent and direct audit," is unfortunately a very rare
occurrence in our times.

We may illustrate the direct observation of the ultimate principal
in Figure 17.

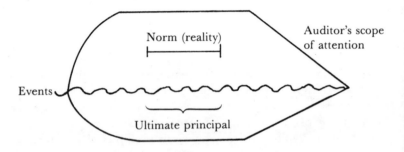

Figure 17

In this scheme we introduced a new concept: the "scope of
attention." The "scope of attention" is the field that the auditor
can view in his memory with proper intensity, so as to allow him
a synopsis of the mental models representing the evidence and
norm systems in order to make a judgment.

Every judgment or opinion presupposes a certain "scope of
attention." If we are unable to keep to mental models in our
memory or if we are unable to have them at the proper level
of intensity in our attention scope, we are unable to judge properly.
We can judge or have an independent opinion only about mental
models (surrogates) at the proper level that can be encompassed
or contained by our "scope of attention."

The limited scope of attention of the human person is only
one of the difficulties of the audit inquiry. The other, and perhaps
more serious, difficulty arises in cases of historical or anticipatory

audits (audits of past evidence or future evidence).

The auditor may have direct access to the area of evidence (the ultimate principal) if he conducts a contemporary audit of some events within his scope of attention. In all the other audits, the events representing the ultimate principal are gone forever or did not happen until the audit, and the auditor had to rely on surrogates at different levels of the data pyramid.

The surrogates might be objects, documents, records, notes, personal representations (witnesses), or, in general, anything that provides data related to the field of the ultimate principal. They are surrogates, and grouped or organized, they provide other secondary, tertiary, and so on, surrogates.

We may define the audit inquiry (procedures to allow a judgment on the truth of the purported evidence) as the sum of procedures necessary to establish the relationship between the surrogates and the ultimate principal of the field of inquiry.

We could consider the ultimate principal, which is indicated by the surrogates purportedly representing the field, as an area (for example, the area of an island or an estate). The auditor receives a group of data, a surrogate, stating that the value of the island or estate is $55,000. The "value of $55,000" is at a very high level of generalization: it is at the top of the data pyramid, the base of which is the ultimate principal, the actual objects on the island or estate at a given moment of time that is already passed (historical audit).

How shall the auditor proceed? His time and effort are limited. The time allowed will be determined by the needs of the decision maker who requires the auditor's opinion (the judgment) and by the changes brought about in the ultimate principal by the passage of time. The effort is determined by the cost of the effort, by the compensation for the energy spent.

To use his time and energy efficiently, the auditor has to plan his procedures. The plan will consist of interrelated individual procedures. The individual procedures, or audit steps, have to be restricted, as they cannot exceed the "scope of attention" of the person performing them. At the conclusion, there will be a judgment establishing the correlations between some part of the ultimate principal and a surrogate or between surrogates at the same or higher level of abstractions.

Surrogates may confirm each other, or they may contradict
each other. An established "true" surrogate may take the place
of a part of the ultimate principal as a principal of higher level.
So the auditor who is following an "audit trail" in the pyramid
of available data or in the pyramid of surrogates may proceed
from judgment to judgment in a chain of judgments at higher
and higher levels in the pyramid until he arrives at the surrogate:
"value $55,000." If the available established surrogates are within
his scope of attention, he will be able to arrive at a judgment
about the truth of this ultimate surrogate.

We may well visualize the audit inquiry as a net thrown over
the data pyramid of the purported structure of evidence. But
the net is not only a cover; it also permeates the body of the
pyramid through connecting links and chains. Each knot in the
net is a subjudgment with an area just big enough to fit the
"scope of attention" of an individual. And the net is not closed
from the outside. It has threads sticking to the outside in order
to allow the perception of the data from the world outside the
data pyramid. The knots in the structures, which are the subjudgments by the auditor or by others delegated by him to make
the subjudgments, establish surrogates of a special quality. We
may call those surrogates "verified surrogates."

As the audit proceeds, more and more surrogates in the data
pyramid become "verified surrogates" or "rejected surrogates."
The area of "rejected surrogates" can be encircled by a network
of "accepted surrogates" and may have no impact on the higher
levels of the network system. The same may happen with areas
of "verified surrogates" if they are encircled or covered by an
area of "rejected surrogates." Some areas may be left blank without
being incorporated into the network. The distance between the
knots may be large or small, but it can never exceed the scope
of the auditor's attention.

The data pyramid is built on the area of the ultimate principal,
but the ultimate principal disappears with time. It leaves only
a layer of ultimate surrogates for posterity, a group of potential
sources of data representing the ultimate principal. The data
pyramid is built on the ultimate surrogates. The auditor constructs
his imaginary network from the level of surrogates that he has
to verify or use for further judgment. In his planning, he has

to work down on the data pyramid by devising his network so that he will reach the ultimate surrogates. He will proceed within the given data pyramid, as well as outside the data pyramid, by planning for the reception of data (surrogates) from the world existing outside the data pyramid.

THE AUDIT STEPS

The individual audit steps are the smallest units in the audit network. We could imagine them as the knots in the pyramid-like structure of the network. They consist of the matching of a surrogate, an individual item of the evidence, to the norm of truth and the resulting judgment. They may be at the lowest level of generalizations, at the bottom of the pyramid, or at a higher level.

In an audit we have to deal with a proposition (surrogate) that is purported to be true. In an investigation we have to establish the actual events without possessing a body of purported evidence.

In an investigation we have to approach every surrogate with the "untrue hypothesis" (null hyphothesis). In an audit we approach the individual surrogates with the "true hypothesis." The reason for the approach by using the true hypothesis is simply pragmatic. The audit procedures are suffering from limitations of time and effort imposed on the auditor. By using the untrue hypothesis, we would be required to gather so many other surrogates (pieces of evidence) that an audit of more comprehensive type would be impossible. Imagine only the audit of the sales transactions of a small firm for a month if we were to assume that all the sales invoices (surrogates) were untrue representations of the transactions they are supposed to record. We may end up by accepting sales invoices as true if they are signed by two witnesses in front of a justice of the peace or a notary public! The signature by two witnessess in front of the justice of the peace would be a quality incorporated in the norm system "truth," against which the surrogate is matched.

The true hypothesis does not imply that we stamp all surrogates automatically as true. To be established as true, the surrogate has to be matched against the norm of truth as it exists in our imagination (memory). It has to meet the requirements set by the norm system; for example, the sales invoice will be matched against our norm system. It has to correspond to our idea of a "true sales invoice at that date and under the conditions existing at that moment."

Let us analyze the norm structure of truth in the case of the sales invoice:

1. *The invoice has to fit into the environment.*
   It fits into the environment if:
   a. It has a form similar to other sales invoices.
   b. It has a serial number and date that fits into the sequence with other invoices.
   c. It is made out in the same form as the other invoices.
   d. It is signed or paraphrased by persons who are authorized to do so.
   e. It describes merchandise or services usually sold by the firm.
   f. The pricing and quantities are within the usual limits.
   g. It went through the control procedures required by the regulations of the firm.
   h. It was stored (filed) in the same way as other similar invoices are stored.
2. *The invoice has to be supported by other surrogates of the underlying principal.*
   Other surrogates might be:
   a. Acknowledgment of the purchase order from the same customer for the same merchandise in quantities and prices identifiable (date and reference) with the same transaction.
   b. Sales order, identifiable with the same transaction.
   c. Delivery slip, identifiable with the same transaction.
   d. Record of receipt of payment, identifiable with the transaction.
   e. Confirmation (verbal or in writing) of the underlying transaction by a witness (a connection to data outside the data pyramid).
3. *There shall be no signs (clues) that the invoice does not fit into the environment or that it is not reconcilable to other surrogates.*

The last requirement (3) of the "truth" norm seems to be a

repetition of the two previous ones. It is, however, nothing else but 1 and 2 stated in a negative way.

The justification for stating requirement 3 independently lies in the extreme importance of the negative features in the audit inquiry. As we approach the surrogates by using the true hypothesis, any clues that would indicate that the surrogate does not represent the purported principal have to be noticed and clarified. A "clue" is anything that helps in the interpretation of data and in the making of inferences from the data. We could also say that a clue is anything that helps in the solution of a problem. Clues are data or groups of data that we can perceive. The danger is that we may miss them without even being aware of their existence. Their existence and importance is discovered sometimes after an unexpected complication or catastrophe.

The clues may appear in one of the surrogates or in the relationship of separate surrogates to each other.

A few years ago a young auditor of the Department of National Revenue audited the books and records of a construction company. He inspected the purchase invoices of the firm. The purchased material and services lost their identity in the construction jobs that the company had finished in the past and in the constructions that were in process. The purchase invoices were properly checked, recorded, and paid. The auditor could not see anything that would indicate that they were not "true." Then, in a flash of insight, he realized that one of the invoices was clean and had not been folded. The other invoices, which had arrived by mail, were folded or were somewhat soiled by the usual handling.

He checked the other invoices that had been received from the same firm. All of them were clean and unfolded. This potential clue prompted him to start an investigation, an activity to establish missing evidence. He did not find the name of the firm in the directory. He checked with the bank where the remittances issued in payment of the invoices had been deposited. The account was in the name of the purported supplier who had sent the invoices, but the only deposits were the remittances from the construction company. And the only person who was authorized to draw checks on the account was the president of the construction company. He withdrew money from the account in order to pay for his personal expenses and investments. The president was faced with the evidence and finally a small printing press was discovered in the basement of his residence.

After the discovery the following evidence was established: The small clerical staff in the office never inspected the material deliveries or the services received and used on the job locations. They simply accepted the invoices that had been approved and acknowledged by the foreman on the location or by the president, who personally supervised the jobs. So it was easy for the president to print invoices and receipt forms in the name of a nonexisting firm. He presented the properly acknowledged and processed invoices to the clerical staff for recording and payment. The president opened an account in a bank in the name of the nonexisting firm, of which he was the only signing officer. Payments were sent directly to the bank. The invoices and receipts were formally correct. If the president had placed the invoices in an envelope, the illegal operations would still have continued.

The key in the inquiry was the clue that invoices purported to be surrogates for a nonexisting principal were "irregular"—they had not been folded. The auditor risked his time and reputation as an efficient worker by deciding to investigate the apparently unimportant discrepancy in the appearance of some invoices.

How many of us experienced auditors would have had the flash of insight in the same situation?

The sales invoice had to correspond to the "truth structure" in order to be verified. The invoice itself is at the nearest level to the ultimate principal, the sales transaction.

We have to develop our illustration further and proceed to a higher level of surrogates in the data pyramid of the firm. The next level could be the sales figure for a time period, let us say for a month.

When do we accept a sales figure of one million dollars for the month of May as "true"? We may attempt to follow the pattern adopted previously in the case of the individual sales invoice. Perhaps it will help; perhaps we will have to modify it:

1. *The sales figure for May has to fit into the environment.*
   The figure fits into the environment if:
   a. It was developed by summarizing the daily sales for the entire month.

b. The recording and the summarizing of daily sales were performed according to the prescribed usual procedures of the firm.

c. The figures appear in the records in the proper place and in the proper sequence.

2. *The sales figure (a surrogate) has to be supported by other surrogates of the underlying principal.*

Supporting surrogates may be at a lower level, nearer to the ultimate principal, or at a level equal in the data pyramid of the firm. Surrogates at a lower level are:

a. Individual sales invoices for the month. If all the individual invoices for May are verified, we may add them. But the summarization of the sales invoices is not an absolute proof. There must be a reasonable guarantee that no sales occurred without being invoiced.

b. Safeguards within the organization to ensure that all stock issues shall be recorded and invoiced. The safeguards do not appear as a formal document. The auditor has to develop his information about the safeguards (internal control) and arrive at a judgment about their adequacy.

Surrogates at an equal level are:

c. The sum of stock issues for the month.

d. Sales figures for the previous and subsequent periods.

e. The pattern of sales in the previous year.

f. Charges to customers for the month.

g. Cash receipts for sales for the month.

h. The pattern of sales per customers.

3. *There shall be no signs (clues) that the sales figure does not fit into the environment or that it is not reconcilable to other surrogates.*

The clues indicating the possibility of an irregularity or an "untruth" of one of the surrogates are of primary importance. The auditor has to develop some surrogates from past operations and from data at a lower level for himself, and he has to use those surrogates in judging about the truth of the other surrogates.

In our firm, when I was a student in accounts, we had as a client a small chain of supermarkets. We were acting as the shareholders' auditor. One of the problems in the audit was the audit of sales for the five stores. The partner in charge of the

audit for us developed an ingenious, although somewhat time-consuming, method of developing surrogates.[2] We received all the
cash register rolls from the stores. The clerical staff in the office
checked every tenth roll for additions and recorded in a schedule
for each store and each cash register the total daily sales, the
number of sales, and the average amount of a sale. After a few
months we could fairly accurately predict the sales for a particular
day of the week and the number of sales to be expected for
the day. For a Wednesday the average amount of each sale was
around $2.50.

The incoming cash register rolls had to fit the established pattern
of previous surrogates and, in fact, they did. But once we came
across a relatively thin roll, which showed average sales on a
Wednesday amounting to over $20. The partner in charge called
the general manager of the client firm and asked him if perhaps
some arrangement had been made to handle institutional sales
on Wednesday through one cash register. There had been no
such arrangements. The management decided to investigate the
matter in order to establish the missing evidence and to explain
the discrepancy in the usual pattern of sales. The general manager
arranged for a confidential surveillance of the cash registers in
the store for the next Wednesday. Everything went as usual during
the day. The cashiers handed over the cash to the store manager;
he took charge of the rolls from the cash registers. He was supposed
to lock the receipts in the safe. But the security man who watched
the store from outside discovered that the store manager went
to one of the cash registers and operated it for about twenty
minutes, producing a roll without actual transactions.

The next morning the general manager and the auditor inspected
the cash to be deposited and there was again the thin roll. It
turned out that the store manager had replaced a real cash register
roll with a new one, which had been prepared by himself and
which showed lesser sales. He never asked the cashiers to sign
for the money that they handed over; he simply signed their
names himself. The girls, trusting him and ignorant of the
requirement, never questioned this practice. In his capacity as
store manager, he had to close the premises. His presence in

---

[2] Paul Greenbloom, CA, Toronto, Ontario, Canada, 1957.

the store without witnesses gave him the opportunity to prepare a phony roll and replace the real one, while pocketing the difference of a few hundred dollars.

Without the sales-control schedule developed by the auditor and without the knowledge of the persons providing the data about sales, the store manager would still have enjoyed his "fringe benefits."

In this case the auditor developed some surrogates of past sales. The consistency of the data displayed by those surrogates established them as possessing the quality of truth and as being indicators of normal operations. A new surrogate showed dramatically different average sales dollars per transaction. The new surrogate had to be reconciled to the established ones. The discrepancy was a clue, and the clue had to be cleared before the data shown by the new surrogate could be accepted as truth.

We can see from this instance that the auditor lends different "truth" or "reliability" qualities to different surrogates.

Some surrogates are more reliable or trustworthy; others are of lesser reliability. We may say that the surrogates have a certain "truth quality."

We are unable to turn back or stop the march of time. A transaction, an event, is gone at the moment it happened. It can be recalled only in the memory of witnesses (or in the memory of others) with the help of surrogates laid down in the form of data.

How can we expect the auditor to be able to establish the truth of a surrogate, a representation, if the underlying ultimate principal is gone for ever? And how could he establish the reality if the underlying ultimate principal was far beyond his individual scope of attention, as, for example, are the thousands of transactions of a medium-sized firm?

We have to assume that certain surrogates are reliable, that they are true, enough to warrant their acceptance as truth. We will agree that humans can remember. If the auditor observes something, focusing his attention on an event, he will accept it as truth or reality in the past. If he produces data (surrogates) about the event when he observed it, he will consider the surrogates as true surrogates of the underlying event (the principal).

He accepts the surrogates as true because he has had continuous awareness of his control over his memory and the supporting other surrogates. But the auditor is only exceptionally in a situation when he is lucky enough to have in his possession self-produced and continuously controlled surrogates. He has to rely on surrogates produced by others. What is the truth quality of those surrogates? When can we accept them, when do we have to question them? The problem deserves further inquiry.

The Truth Value of the Surrogates

The surrogates represent groups of data from which the receiver intends and tries to rebuild in his imagination some aspects of an event or several events. At this point we have to refer back to "Psychology of Information" (Chapter III). In his procedures to establish the truth of a purported evidence, the auditor is in the position to evoke data or groups of data (surrogates) available in the world around him. He is the final receiver and user of certain data. He has to overcome the obstacles in the communication process discussed earlier in our text.

These obstacles are:

1. *Data may not be perceived.*
2. *Data may be perceived incorrectly.*
3. *Data may be incorrectly interpreted.*
4. *Data correctly interpreted may result in incorrect inferences.*

The auditor is on the receiving end of the communication process in his search for the surrogates. He has the difficult task of ascertaining that he perceives the necessary data appearing as surrogates. He can perceive the existing surrogates if they are presented (communicated) to him as the result of a decision made by others to present the data. So one group of surrogates is presented to him. But the question is, Who are the persons presenting the surrogates?

If the sources of surrogates pursue the same goals in the audit as the auditor does, the surrogates controlled and presented by them have more probability of truth than if the surrogates come from sources controlled by persons having different goals (purposes) from the auditor.

Surrogates are controlled by the persons controlling the sources of the surrogates. We may imagine for ourselves that the surrogates possess a certain quality (for example, color). Surrogates originating from one primary source may be considered "blue surrogates." Another independent witness may give a different or similar testimony (primary surrogate) of the event under review. This testimony may be considered a "yellow surrogate." Surrogates originating from the same primary sources maintain their basic color (quality) even if they are developed into surrogates of a higher order.

Surrogates have more truth value if they are of mixed color quality. If three or four independent eyewitnesses provide data about an event, the auditor will be able to reconstruct a model of the event (the ultimate principal). This model, as a surrogate, will carry the combined colors of "blue," "yellow," and "green," indicating the different sources. If two witnesses who provided data are not independent from each other but have discussed the events, their testimony as a surrogate has to be considered to possess similar but not quite identical colors.

As a general rule, we may say that surrogates having a single color (controlled by a single person or group of persons) are less reliable than those having a variety of colors. In other words, surrogates controlled by persons or groups having different potential motives and goals are more valuable than single-colored surrogates.

The need for surrogates derived from sources that are not controlled by the same sources makes it necessary for the auditor to have access to surrogates from different sources. The auditor has to know the reality represented by the pyramid of data (surrogates) and the surrounding areas of the reality. Naturally, he will probably never be able to observe the ultimate principal except in a contemporary audit. But he has to have a fair exposure to similar, analogous areas of the reality. If I want to audit a statement about mice in a room, I have to possess a fair amount of knowledge about mice, their behavior, and the room itself with all the furniture and fixtures. Otherwise I will not be in the position to perceive data (surrogates) necessary to establish the evidence. I will miss data, and I will be unable to find clues. In addition to being exposed to similar realities, the auditor has to be in the position to trace the surrogates back to the ultimate principal.

The distance of surrogates from the ultimate principal and the control of surrogates by persons who provide them cannot be established without a fair understanding of the circumstances surrounding the generation of surrogates.

In Chapter III, we discussed the control of communication and information by the originator of the data. The auditor is a receiver and user of the data. He wants to develop the proper information from the groups of data. Perhaps it will be useful to inquire into his role as receiver of data. What can he do to ascertain that he has made the proper inferences from the groups of data serving as surrogates?

The following possibilities were mentioned as ways to facilitate the understanding of data and the correctness of the inferences made:

1. *Preliminary arrangements,* as proper training or "programming," are one possibility. The auditor has to be an expert in the realities surrounding the operations to be audited. He has to understand the people involved, and he has to be active in the area. He has to be aware of the existing surrogates, and he has to have access to additional surrogates outside an existing formal data pyramid, for example, a firm.

Operations at areas to be audited have to be organized so that an audit trail consisting of a series of surrogates will be available. If there are no surrogates, there is no possibility of conducting an audit.

The auditor has to have the necessary authority to select his own surrogates. He cannot be restricted in the selection of surrogates nor in his investigation in case of clues that indicate the "untruth" of one or more surrogates.

The auditor naturally has to have the time and energy necessary to establish the truth of the purported evidence. He needs physical freedom to make the necessary direct observations, and he needs a place in which to keep his confidential notes and schedules.

2. The originator of the communication process has to *use signs, symbols, and words that are familiar to the receiver in the meaning familiar to him.* The auditor as the user of data has to possess the necessary knowledge to interpret and understand the data that appear as surrogates. He has to be an expert not only in the usual signs, symbols, and words that appear as surrogates

but also in the way that those signs are used and in the way that they are supposed to appear. Irregularity in their use is a clue that they represent something different and not the principal that they are purported to represent.

3. The originator of the communication process has to *supply an adequate quantity of data.* The auditor, in the process of establishing the truth of the purported evidence, has to use an adequate number of surrogates. The net of verified surrogates is not supposed to be incoherent or too loose. "Adequate quantity" of surrogates does not mean a large number of surrogates at the same level having the same "color of control," as, for example, a multitude of sales invoices. It means an "adequate quantity" of surrogates at different levels in the data pyramid and "controlled" by different sources.

Naturally those surrogates have to exist. Eventually the auditor has to create additional surrogates to enable himself to verify a complex pyramid of data. The surrogates have to exist not only about the ultimate principal of the data pyramid but also from the side of the "reality." An auditor who never heard the sound of a trumpet will be unable to verify a sound purported to be the sound of a trumpet unless he relies on the opinion of experts.

We used the expression "adequate quantity of surrogates." An "adequate quantity" is settled by legal, professional standards. In other cases, the problem is left with the auditor, and he has to decide it according to his own personal standards.

4. The originator of data in a communication process has to *organize data in groups, facilitating the desired interpretation and inferences to be made.* The auditor on the receiving end of the multiple communications has to organize the surrogates, too. But his organization is based on a different classification. He has to determine the level of the pyramid of surrogates on which he has to rely and report. This level could be the "Financial Position" level in the case of statutory audit or the level of the individual characteristics as stated by the Criminal Code in the case of the judge's audit of the purported event.

The surrogates at the desired level will be tied to the ultimate principal by a chain of surrogates. The shorter the chain, the easier the audit.

It is the auditor's task to organize the surrogates in the proper chain and in appropriate "color groups," depending on their origin. In the resulting network, he may have some surrogates above the desired level, and he may have some missing areas of single-colored surrogates. By reviewing the structure of surrogates, the auditor has to follow certain principles in deciding upon the weight to be given to them:

a. *Surrogates originating from expert sources carry more weight than surrogates from unqualified sources.* But the surrogates originating from expert sources cannot be accepted automatically. The expert's qualifications, his motivation, and the way he acquired the data resulting in the surrogates have to be classified before there can be an unconditional acceptance of the surrogates. Equally important are the conditions under which the expert produced the surrogates. Did he know that the surrogates produced by him would serve the purposes of a special audit?

Most of today's audits are team efforts. In a team audit, the person who signs the audit report is the key man. He could be considered the sole auditor, while the other persons who provide him with information (surrogates) for his final decision on the problem of verifications are more or less expert witnesses who perform the gathering of surrogates and present their own opinions, in the form of new surrogates, to the top person in the team.

In this last, or top, phase of the audit, the auditor who is in charge of the final opinion has to proceed along the same lines as the persons who verified sales invoices and monthly sales figures in our previous example:

(1) He will see *how the surrogates fit into the environment.* He has to survey the notes, the working papers produced by his staff members (the expert witnesses). He will take the contents of the surrogates presented to him, and he will reconcile them with surrogates developed by himself from last year's working papers or from any other sources.

(2) Next, he has to *consider the surrogates in the light of other surrogates presented or available to him about the same area of "underlying principal."* He has to review the surrogates produced by other members of his staff or by outsiders (confirmations, explanations). One of the main purposes of this review is to determine the

sources of surrogates. How far are they from the ultimate principal? Who controlled their content before they became available to the auditors? What is the "color mix" of the surrogates?

(3) And throughout this activity he has to *look for clues or indications that there is a discrepancy between the forms and contents of the surrogates and the realities of the underlying principal.* In case of doubt, he will order or perform an investigation, a search for evidence to clear the perceived or suspected discrepancies.

b. *Surrogates from unqualified sources provide more clues than surrogates from well-qualified (expert) sources.* Surrogates from expert sources may be dangerous. Persons who know the purposes of the audit may (intentionally or unintentionally) distort the representation of the underlying principal. Their expertise or skill may develop into routine handling of the events (the underlying principal). Sometimes the surrogates provided by them are based on motives that are in conflict with the purposes of the audit.

They may develop surrogates from evidence that is satisfactory for their purposes but which would not be enough for the auditor who has different requirements in his audit. Surrogates provided by experts usually do not contain clues that could raise doubt as to the "truth content" of the underlying principal. Experts make their own conclusions about clues and discrepancies if they know the other surrogates.

On the other hand, the representations (surrogates) of less qualified or unqualified persons are usually less subject to distortions, especially if they are direct, primary surrogates. An unqualified person is usually not aware of the implications. His own conclusions might be "not to the point" or "irrelevant." But the surrogates originated by him may disclose important clues and discrepancies between surrogates and the underlying principal.

I remember a young lady on our audit team in Toronto. She used to go to lunch with the secretaries and female employees of our clients. If we had a touchy internal-control problem or some other audit problem of a confidential nature, we used to ask her to get some information from the "girls." She usually had the answer in two or three days. Our approach was perhaps unprofessional but it was efficient, and it produced excellent and reliable results.

c. *The shorter the distance between the ultimate principal and the*

surrogates, the higher the reliability ("truth value") of the surrogates.
The term "distance" in the above statement has two meanings.
It may be understood as distance in time. It is a commonplace
that subsequent impulses push out old memories. The human
memory may retain schemata, pictures, models of events, and
conclusions. With the passing of time and under the impact of
new impulses, the contents of the memory fade away or sometimes
even change. With the passing of time, not only the human
memories fade away but also objects or traces left by events are
changed or annihilated. So the field of available surrogates becomes
more and more restricted.

Old surrogates are subject to errors in interpretations, errors
in references. It is more difficult to trace them to their originator.
It is impossible to establish who actually controlled the surrogates
(the color of the surrogate), and it is difficult to provide supporting
surrogates. After a time a big lie may become truth, especially
if it is repeated often enough. We have seen it in our times,
as the big lies of the 1920s, 1930s, and 1940s are accepted as
truth even by young scholars.

The second interpretation of the term "distance" is that of the
"geographical" distance in the data pyramid. The ultimate principal
is first represented by a primary surrogate, as, for example, the
report of an eyewitness. The primary surrogate may serve as
principal for a surrogate: the report of somebody who read the
story by the eyewitness. And soon a chain of surrogates comes
into existence, the new surrogates getting farther and farther away
from the ultimate principal. Naturally, reductions in content
changes in emphasis, and distortions in the communication process
result, even without intentional slanting by the persons involved.

It is almost a truism that the truth value of a surrogate decreases
with every instance of communications.

The primary surrogates are the first reductions of the ultimate
principal. They are constructed to serve as data in a communication
process. As such, they are subject to certain constraints: they are
shaped to fulfill a certain purpose (the purpose of the resulting
first communication process); they are constructed to provide
information to a certain receiver or group of receivers. The
originator of primary surrogates has an actual receiver in mind
when he is shaping his message. The actual receiver has some

knowledge about the circumstances, perhaps even about the event. He possesses some attitudes, a structure of schemata, perhaps anticipated by the producer of the primary surrogates.

The primary surrogates will be received, interpreted, and understood by the producer of secondary surrogates. He will draw inferences from the primary surrogates, and he will incorporate the information into his memory. The secondary surrogate may be produced immediately upon receipt of the primary one or later. If it is produced later, the memory of the originator may be strengthened by written notes, records, and so forth, or it may be left without support. He again is placed in a specific communication role. His communication will have a purpose; it will be subject to limitations of time, errors, and noise. He will have a specific receiver in mind by constructing the data, the secondary surrogates.

The process will be repeated with every instance of communications. Therefore the reliability and representative value of the surrogates are decreasing with every step of communications.

But more distant receivers of surrogates in the communication process may be in the possession of more than one surrogate. Some of those may be primary, others secondary, and so forth. They may be able to build a closer picture of some attributes of the ultimate principal than can a direct witness who did not concentrate on the attributes in question. The different surrogates coming from independent chains of communications may reinforce each other, complement each other. We could call this phenomenon the "stereo effect" or "confirmation effect" of surrogates. Naturally, the surrogates have to come from different sources. The sources should be independent from the level of ultimate principal. If the surrogates from independent sources cannot be reconciled, we may find errors or intentional distortions in the chain of communications.

We shall not forget that sometimes the formally independent surrogates are independent only in their last appearance; they may originate, not independently at the ultimate principal level, but from a higher level, from a primary or secondary surrogate as common source for all of them. An example of those surrogates is that of indirect witnesses who heard a story from the same eyewitness of an event.

The surrogates which appear to be independent may be interdependent. They may be influenced by each other in their process of birth. The eyewitnesses might have discussed an event. They can provide primary surrogates, but those surrogates are also secondary ones, as the witness produced them not only from the ultimate principal but also from additional surrogates of representations by persons with whom he had discussed the accident. Surrogates may be, and we may say that this is so in most cases, of mixed origin. Therefore, the tracing of surrogates to the ultimate principal is not an easy task. A typical example of a surrogate that cannot be traced back to the ultimate principal is "hearsay" evidence.

Naturally the auditor has to weigh the probable truth value of a surrogate. The probable truth value is the relationship to the ultimate principal. The tracing of the relationship is sometimes very difficult in view of the distance between the surrogate and the ultimate principal, as discussed above. The establishment of the probable truth value requires a judgment.

In this judgment the norms applied should be the criteria of truth or reality, but they are unknown. Therefore, the auditor is unable to use them as norms or criteria for his judgment. He has to replace them by norms that are available. The available norm system has the following categories:

(1) *Acceptable* as representing probable truth because the surrogate is not remote from the ultimate principal and the source is reliable.

(2) *Perhaps acceptable* as representing probable truth because the surrogate is not remote from the ultimate principal but the reliability of the source is questionable.

(3) *Perhaps acceptable* as representing probable truth because the surrogate, although remote, does originate from a reliable source.

(4) *Not acceptable* as representing probable truth because the surrogate is remote and has passed through unreliable sources.

Naturally the resulting judgment is only an interim judgment. The judgment will be reexamined in the light of interim judgments passed on the available surrogates. We may say that those interim judgments pertain to the formal character of the surrogates. A surrogate's contents may be accepted as truth, even if the formal character of the surrogate is defective and would be rejected, unless several other surrogates of impeccable formal characteristics indicate the same traits or features of the ultimate principal.

The terms "remoteness of the surrogate from the ultimate principal," "reliability of the source," and "probable truth" are rather indefinite, and they may be interpreted differently in each individual situation. We have no certain yardstick for the measurement of remoteness, reliability, and probable truth. We may even argue that they are too vague to be meaningful. But it is in the interpretation of those terms in the cases of actual judgment that the experience, personal character, and intellectual character of the auditor shows.

Another important feature in the interpretation of the concepts of remoteness and reliability is the element of the danger or risk involved in the audit. The element of danger is a function of the purpose of the audit. Every audit has a purpose (goal). The purpose of the audit is determined by the various needs of an underlying decision-making process. If the risk of incorrect decisions due to errors in audit and untrue audit judgments (opinions) is great, the auditor will narrow the range of acceptability of a surrogate by restricting the concepts of reliability, probability, and remoteness.

The risk involved in the use of the audit opinion or judgment plays an important part not only in the weighing of the formal character of the surrogates but also in the interpretation of the contents of the surrogates and especially in the scope of the inferences drawn from them. The higher the risk involved and the higher the interest in the audit, the stricter the interpretation of the data groups represented by the surrogates and the narrower the scope of possible inferences.

d. *The reconcilable contents of surrogates confirm the reliability of the sources.* If the surrogates possess weak formal character—as, for example, the surrogates from unqualified or distant sources which contain representations that are identical or partly identical to other independent surrogates of strong formal character—the reliability of otherwise weak sources is enhanced.

We can analyze the surrogates according to their formal character and according to their contents. For the truth value or the usefulness of the surrogates in the audit process, the content of the surrogates is more important than their formal character.

Formally defective surrogates may present important clues and therefore cannot be omitted without inquiry.

In judicial procedures, due to the very high interest involved (for example, the life or freedom of a person), hearsay evidence is not admissible. The judge will not even admit its presentation. But in an audit the auditor cannot disregard it. He has to attempt to reconcile the hearsay evidence with the contents of other surrogates from more reliable sources. The reconciliation may provide clues and disclose areas that need to be investigated.

CHAPTER VII
AUDIT AND INVESTIGATION

WE MADE THE DISTINCTION earlier between the audit process and the investigation. The audit process is the evaluation of purported evidence, while the investigation is a process to establish missing evidence.

In the actual audit the auditor may often find a need to search for missing evidence, as some of the surrogates representing the purported evidence may not be reconcilable or may contain clues that have to be cleared.

So, parts of an audit process in actual life may take the character of an investigation. On the other hand, an investigation that results in the establishment of an ultimate principal (the facts) is defective without a subsequent audit, a verification by the investigator himself.

The ASOBAC (Report of the Committee on Basic Auditing Concepts, AAA, 1972) makes no distinction between the audit inquiry (the reconciliation with each other of surrogates that represent the purported evidence and of surrogates that are available to the auditor from other sources) and the investigation (the search for surrogates to establish missing evidence).[1] They are both called the "Investigative Process."

There are important differences in the approach and methodology between the procedures that the auditor uses in the verification of a surrogate and in the search for surrogates; therefore, the refinement in terminology is both warranted and useful.

In an investigation, every potential surrogate is valuable. The investigator has no purported model of evidence available. He is using in his work the "null hypothesis." He may come across a surrogate or a potential surrogate, a clue of very weak formal

---

[1] "Report of the Committtee on Basic Auditing Concepts," *Accounting Review*, Supplement (Sarasota, Fla., 1972), pp. 15–76.

character. He will build up a tentative hypothesis as part of the potential model of the "truth," a past event. The hypothesis will not be accepted as truth until the investigator can find enough surrogates confirming the contents of his hypothesis. Since an investigator lacks the surrogates that will allow him to establish the evidence model, he has to disregard the "formal characteristics" in the initial stages of his work. He has to rely on his imagination and his memory in devising potential sources of surrogates.

This is a time-consuming process, and it requires energy. Because of the interrelationships between the audit and investigation process and because of the importance of the investigative procedures within an audit, we have to discuss the investigation process in more detail.

INVESTIGATION—AN ILLUSTRATION

We shall examine the structure of an investigation and the procedures used in an investigation process by discussing a "simple" police investigation of a murder case.

A corpse was found in one of the lanes downtown. A passerby came across the corpse and called the police station. The duties of the police include the prosecution of offenders against the law. There is a possibility that foul play was involved in the death of the person whose body was found, so the "investigation squad" was dispatched immediately to the location.

We find in this situation a surrogate—the phone call to the police station. The surrogate may represent an ultimate principal, an eventual murder (an event). Murder is an indictable offense under the Criminal Code. To disregard the phone call as a "childish prank" would be risky; therefore, action was taken to establish the "truth" of the surrogate (phone call) and to find the "interim principal" (the corpse).

We can assume that the corpse was there in the lane. The investigating team will immediately look for additional new surrogates on the location. Before it is taken to the morgue, members of the team will inspect the corpse for determination of the cause of death. If they find signs of death by violence, they will make a thorough search for traces of blood, for signs of a fight, for objects that could be connected to the events.

The corpse itself is the link between the different potential surrogates. One surrogate may lead to others: the clothing of the victim, the contents of his pockets, his wallet, his name, his address—all are valuable new surrogates. If they know the victim's name, they can find his next of kin and his friends. They can furnish information on his life style.

The search for surrogates at the initial stages of an investigation is directed outward. We may consider the corpse as the center point. Attempts to gather additional potential surrogates could be considered as being directed from the center to the peripheries in every conceivable direction. The data collected are potential surrogates in their relationships to the ultimate principal: the events leading to and culminating in the death of the victim. The execution of the investigation process at this first expansionary stage pre-supposes the familiarity with the prevailing conditions on the location. Customs, habits, and attitudes of people have to be well known by the person in charge of data collection. For persons experienced in the city, the task will be easy. For a policeman from another country, it would be cumbersome, difficult, and almost impossible.

The investigation at this first stage is a search for surrogates using the available surrogate. The investigator interprets the available surrogate in light of his stored knowledge of the environment, and he makes tentative inferences which are directed toward the discovery of other related surrogates. His mind will follow either schemata established by experience or similarities tentatively arrived at in his imagination.

When sufficient numbers of surrogates are collected, some of them will fall into a certain pattern—a "model" or structure—and parts of the underlying ultimate principal may be cleared up. The surrogates collected about the corpse may indicate the victim's name, his pattern of life, his friends and, perhaps, his enemies, too. We may consider the process as similar to that of mapping an unknown territory. The starting point may be an elevation. From this elevation we can determine the relative position and elevation of other points in the territory. The series of data (surrogates) will fall into a pattern, and a range of hills or mountains can be drawn up on the map.

After the first structures of the surrogates emerge, we arrive at the second stage of the investigation process: the model-building or hypothesis stage.

To go on and simply accumulate additional data without any direction would be time-consuming, costly, and inefficient. The emerging patterns (submodels) indicate the dark undiscovered areas, the connecting links between the apparent substructures of surrogates. In this stage the attention of the investigator is directed to the discovery of surrogates that could tie together the submodels and establish the ultimate principal. I call this stage the "hypothesis stage" because the investigator has to assume certain possible shapes of the events that constitute the ultimate principal and direct his work to find surrogates that either support or invalidate his assumptions.

The additional data may enrich the surrogate groups already established, may invalidate some of them, or may turn out to be irrelevant; that is, they may not be surrogates at all. Finally, the total structure of surrogates may be established, indicating, with more or less probability, the ultimate principal.

The third stage of the investigation process is the "confirmation stage." In this stage, one of the several hypotheses structuring the available data becomes prominent, and the attention is directed toward the finding of the missing surrogates which would confirm the predominant and tentatively accepted hypothesis about the ultimate principal.

In our illustration of the murder investigation started by a phone call about a corpse, the police established the identity of the victim, his habits, his friends, and his enemies in the first stage of the investigation. In the second stage the search was directed toward clearing up several hypotheses: (1) robbery and murder, (2) dispute and murder, (3) slaying without a motive by a maniac, (4) murder for revenge, and so forth.

Finally, the personal effects of the victim may turn up in the possession of a man who was seen with him shortly before the time of his death; the hypothesis of robbery and murder by that person is confirmed, and thus the structure (pyramid) of surrogates is complete.

The fourth and last stage of the investigation process is the audit of the final findings. The surrogates organized into the information pyramid have to be reviewed, apparent contradictions reconciled, and the ultimate principal established as "true." This is usually achieved by the confession of the suspected murderer, testimony of witnesses, and so forth.

Investigation is a heuristic process designed to discover something that is not yet proposed or asserted (*heuriskein* is a Greek word meaning "to find").[2] Audit is the process of the evaluation of something proposed or asserted.

We illustrated a police-oriented investigation and identified four distinct phases in the investigation process. One of the phases was the audit phase. The four phases are not discernible in a more complex investigation. The initial groups of surrogates may allow the investigator to make several models or hypotheses, and the result could be a dead end, a situation in which no further clues are available in the search for further surrogates.

We may say that audit and investigation are as inseparable as our two legs. Together they allow us to approach our goal.

It is easy to analyze the investigation process and to break it down into four phases. It is equally easy to describe or illustrate a successful investigation; but it is difficult to perform an investigation successfully and efficiently.

The first area of difficulty is to identify in the ever-changing and infinite world around us the surrogates that relate to the desired ultimate principal. The world around us supplies us with millions of data that may be surrogates, but we don't see the connections between them and the desired ultimate principal.

Samuel Leeuwenhoek's microscope was used as a toy by interested scientists for almost two and one-half centuries, until Louis Pasteur made the proper inferences between some little creatures observed through the microscope and the fermentation process of the vine. Once he had established the ties between the presence of some bacteria and the fermentation process of the vine, it was relatively easy for him to find a connection between the presence of other microscopic forms and the fermentation process of milk. Reading Pasteur's papers, Robert Koch, with a "flash of insight," discovered the connections between the presence of other microscopic creatures in the blood of deceased animals and their fatal diseases.

[2] *The American Heritage Dictionary of the English Language*, ed. W. Morris (New York: American Heritage Publishing Co., 1969), s.v. "heuristic."

His insight opened up the minds of his colleagues, and the modern medical sciences came into existence.

Experience is a word implying skill, capacity, or ability gained by a person which enables him to anticipate and expect certain similarities between structural connections of certain data. By participation or direct observance, we acquire certain information which is organized in schemata in our memory. Similar structures of data or circumstances evoke in our memory the same schemata, and we become sensitive to the possibility of similar structural connections. We may acquire vicarious experience by learning or reading.

The search for surrogates is always based on analogies, structural hypotheses that are confirmed or not confirmed by past experience. The "flash of insight" is a successful hypothesis. Therefore, experience is only useful if it is coupled with an active imagination, a creative fantasy, or an ability to use the experience vicariously in new situations.

INVESTIGATION OF THE FUTURE—PLANNING

The four phases of the investigation process can be found not only in past-oriented (historical) investigations but also in future-oriented ones. In a future-oriented investigation the goal of the investigator is to anticipate a principal that is not in existence when the investigation is undertaken but which will exist at a given future time. Perhaps it seems strange to speak about a prediction of the future and the establishment of a past event as similar experiences. The only difference between the two is the time factor. In a prediction the ultimate principal is not available, just as it is not available in a past-oriented investigation. In the case of the prediction the surrogates are available at the time of the prediction, and the ultimate principal will be available whether we want it or not. The problem here is to recognize the surrogates, just as in a past-oriented investigation. The problem is made more difficult in the case of a prediction by the possible emergence of events that could render all anticipated surrogates invalid from one moment to another. These events are unforeseen or unexpected.

In retrospect, in an evaluation of validity of the prediction model after the ultimate principal is known and after it has been compared to the prediction model, it is easy to point out the corresponding and divergent features of the two. It is then just as easy to find the real past surrogates and connect them to the anticipated surrogates. (Hindsight is easy wisdom.) Naturally, the longer the time span between the establishment of a surrogate and the future principal, the bigger the risk of the prediction's validity. The risk can be reduced by control if the control over future events can more or less eliminate unexpected changes in the circumstances. The nature of the objects of the prediction is also a factor. I can predict that a building will stand at its present location one year from now because I see the building (a surrogate for the future building) today. But it would be foolish to predict that a car observed today will be parked at the same location next year on the same calendar day. We may acknowledge that different groups in the world surrounding us possess a certain inherent coefficient of change. The risk of change can be expressed in the following simplified formula:

$$\text{Risk of change} = T^2 \times Q \times \frac{1}{C}$$

where T stands for time, Q for the coefficient of change, and C for the planner's control over the event.

The shorter the time span between the unexpected event and the moment of prediction and the lower the coefficient of change, the higher the probability for a correct prediction. The level of control over the components of the future event has a reciprocal effect on the risk of change due to an unforeseen and unexpected event.

The establishment of the future is an investigation having as its purpose the construction of a future situation, event, or environment from surrogates that are available today. The principal in this case is a future principal.

As in every investigation, the investigation of the future can be regarded as consisting of four distinct phases:

1. The search for surrogates (expansion).
2. Establishment of the possible models of the future principal.

3. The search for additional surrogates to validate or negate the various hypotheses (confirmation stage).
4. Audit (validation) of the future principal.

In phase 1, the search for surrogates of a future principal has to be based on the assumption that some component parts of the future principal are available today and that those components will not change significantly in time. Those components include physical and political environment, existence of certain institutions and persons, and so forth.

The investigation of the future is naturally directed by a goal or purpose. Let us assume that our purpose is to devise a master plan to achieve a certain desired situation in the future with the help of the master plan, a budget or a program. The master plan consists of a group of activities or acts which will result in a situation that is inherent in a broader environment of the future. The future principal is the broad area in the future, and within the future principal we can distinguish a narrower field that can be influenced and controlled by an activity or by a chain of activities performed in the time lag running between today and the date of the future principal.

Usually the purpose itself indicates the area in which the present data (the surrogates of the future principal) are developed by considering other surrogates and by inference, anticipating their mutual effects during the time between today and the event of the future principal.

Phase 2 of the investigation of the future is the model-building, the tentative determination of the expected future or expected futures. The data available today on the future are naturally limited. In hindsight we may easily find the missing and unavailable surrogates, but looking ahead, our view is limited to our experience in the area, as it is alive in our memory.

In phase 3 the structures of the expected futures are compared. The comparison may show the need for additional surrogates. The additional surrogates are explored and, if available, used. By inference the surrogates are reconciled, and the expected future principal is established with more or less probability.

The goals of the planning process are important in deciding the necessary details in the future principal. Naturally the forecast of the detailed principal is more difficult and uncertain.

In phase 4 the tentatively established future principal is audited.

We have defined auditing as an evaluation process (a comparison) to ascertain the conformity of a representation (an act or event) to certain norms or criteria, resulting in an opinion (judgment). How can we audit a representation of the future? What norms (criteria) can we use to arrive at an opinion? We will discuss this in some detail.

It is clear that the audit of the future is not verification, as we cannot establish the truth or validity of the representation (a system of surrogates) about something that is not in existence. We can verify only past or present evidence. The audit of the future is a "decision" audit.

THE AUDIT OF THE FUTURE PRINCIPAL

The conceptual structure of the audit of a representation about a future situation or event (a future principal) is identical to that of a representation of something that existed or happened in the past. The evidence consists of a data pyramid, a network of surrogates indicating an ultimate principal. The ultimate principal of the past is gone; it will never return. We only possess more or fewer surrogates about it, in the traces left in the memory of individuals, in records laid down to serve as surrogates, or in events caused by it.

We could be in the possession of surrogates indicating a future principal, just as surrogates indicate the past existence of a principal. We may also misinterpret the surrogate of past principals, we may arrive at incorrect inferences from the surrogates about the past, and we may make errors in judgment or opinion about the past. What is really the difference between the audit of the past and the audit of a representation of the future (a forecast)?

We have to look at the availability and the character of the surrogates available in both cases in order to understand the differences in the two types of audit. In developing the audit steps we arrived at certain requirements with respect to the surrogates and their natures.

We stated that "surrogates originating from expert sources carry more weight than surrogates from unqualified sources" (p. 138).

Is there a "qualified source" of surrogates for a future principal? Is there a person who knows the future? It is almost a triviality to answer this question. But although nobody knows the future, some events or situations of the future can be controlled to some extent by an individual or some individuals who are committed to some action that will or may produce an intended situation or event unless an unforeseen and therefore uncontrollable "cause" gives a different direction to the chain connecting the actual situation in the future to the present representation of it. (In management we may speak about the "umbrella of control" over the events.)

The future principal may be divided into two distinct areas: an uncontrollable area, which is beyond the control of a planner, and a controllable area, which is more or less subject to the control of a person or group of persons.

I make the statement, "Tomorrow at 9 A.M., I shall be in my office at the university." In this representation the future principal is a situation at 9 A.M. in my office. Both the place and time are of uncontrollable nature, as their existence or nonexistence is beyond my control. The situation includes the presence of my person at 9 A.M. in my office. My presence is within my control. I have to get up in time to get dressed and drive to the office in order to be there at 9 A.M. The advent of 9 A.M. tomorrow and the existence of my office at that time are beyond my control. But the character of those two areas in the future principal is stable. According to our past experience, the arrival of tomorrow is certain, and the existence of my office twenty-four hours from now is almost certain. The office could be destroyed by an earthquake or fire, but the coefficient of the occurrence of a disaster is very low. Other uncontrollable events that could prevent me from being in the office at the desired time are numerous. I could be unable to reach the office because I become sick, I oversleep, my car breaks down, there is an unforeseen traffic jam, I get involved in an accident, and so on. The uncontrollable events may be predictable or known in advance, as, for example, the usual traffic jam conditions in the morning. If so, the person in control of the planning and execution can anticipate them. It is more difficult if they are unpredictable, for example, a stalled car or an accident.

If I make the representation that I will be in my office two years from now at 9 A.M., the probability of the validity of the representation is much lower. The time lag between the surrogate and the future principal is too long. We cannot be in possession of surrogates that could preclude an unexpected change in the future principal. The level of control disappears over events in the time span of two years. The occurrence of unforeseen events for which we could not possess surrogates would make the representation's validity questionable, almost improbable.

Now we have to consider the audit of the representation, the evaluation of the validity or probable validity of the representation about the future, the evaluation of the relationship between the present surrogate and the future principal.

In the description of the audit steps, we classified them under three major headings:

1. The auditor has to see how the surrogates about the ultimate principal fit into the environment. The surrogates about the future principal which are available today have to be reconciled to surrogates available about a broader future principal, the environment. The environment surrounds the ultimate future principal.

As an illustration, let us consider the usual yearly operating budget of a business organization. The budget is a plan of action to achieve certain goals of the organization. In preparing a budget, certain assumptions have been made about the future. Some parts of the future, which are controllable by the promoters of the future principal, will be available to the auditor. The firm will provide him with the list and description of the expressly made assumptions in preparing the budget.

The auditor has to look for surrogates from other sources about the anticipated future environment in which the firm will operate. As planned, we may consider the budget to be a pyramid of data about the future principal. In the first group of audit steps, the auditor looks for connections or relationships between the surrogates within the presented data pyramid and those outside the presented structure. He may find no relationships preventing the advent of the ultimate future principal. In the past-oriented audit such a correspondence enhances the "truth value" of a surrogate within the given pyramid of data. In the audit of the future principal the situation is somewhat different.

In the past-oriented audit to establish the truth of the evidence (a verification), the auditor makes inferences from the surrogates or groups of surrogates. He interprets the surrogates and, by inference, makes a judgment about the correspondence of the purported evidence (a purported principal) and the inferred ultimate principal. His judgment will be negative if the surrogates do not correspond to the purported evidence. The past events survive only in their surrogates, but the contents of the surrogates and the quantity of the surrogates is once and for all determined by the past events.

In the search for a future principal we know that the available surrogates are uncertain as to content and that some potential surrogates are not even available. The surrogates about unforeseen events may not even exist at the time of the audit, or even if they do exist, we cannot recognize them as such. Depending on the time span and the nature of the future principal, the occurrence of unforeseen changes in the future is more or less certain. Therefore, the positive verification of the future principal ("it will be so") is impossible, while the positive verification ("it was so") is possible.

On the other hand, the auditor could infer from surrogates available today that the advent of a future principal is either impossible or improbable. He may come across surrogates indicating that the budget of a firm cannot be implemented because some financial commitments were not taken into consideration, because equipment or labor are not available, or because the products have become obsolete. In the audit of a future principal, the negative aspect of the surrogates is more important.

Negative surrogates are naturally important in every audit. But in a past-oriented audit their meaning can be clarified either by investigating additional surrogates, if they are available, or by investigating the areas of apparent differences. The investigation of differences between contradictory surrogates about future principals is more difficult because of the possible occurrences of unforeseen and unexpected events.

2. In our discussion we had already entered into the domain of the second area of the audit steps: *namely, the reconciliation of available surrogates about the ultimate surrogate.* We have mentioned

that some surrogates will be missing in a future-oriented audit; therefore, a positive affirmative verification of the future is impossible. If surrogates indicate the occurrence of events that would prevent the advent of the purported future principal, the auditor could come up with a definite negation of the purported future principal.

3. The third area of the audit is to *look for clues that would indicate something unusual about the surrogates*, thus rendering their "truth value" questionable.

In the audit of a future principal, the clues are of lesser importance, as the truth value of every surrogate is subject to assumptions that cannot be tested. But if the clues show that the occurrence of the future principal is impossible, their importance is decisive.

In summary, the audit of a future principal is restricted to the verification of the present state of affairs. If the present state of affairs (a surrogate for the future principal) contains no features that render the occurrence of the future principal impossible or improbable, the auditor may state so in his opinion. But an absolute statement about the certainty of the future principal is impossible. On the other hand, a negative opinion stating that the future principal will not occur as planned or that it is improbable that it will occur is possible.

In our daily lives and in the management of institutions, we have to rely on representations about the future. But inherent in this reliance is the element of risk about the future. The auditor's function is to reduce the risks in reliance on data and representations.

Operational auditors may devise ingenious methods to simulate the future principal by a model, thereby making it more verifiable. In our illustration of a future-oriented audit, we discussed the operational audit of a new process that had been successfully applied under laboratory conditions. The question was: Will it work under existing plant conditions?

The operational auditor built the model of the actual plant in the laboratories. He simulated the actual plant on a reduced scale. Under laboratory conditions, he actually observed the process, as it was performed concurrently with his observation.

He transformed the future audit into a contemporary or present audit. And his conclusion that the process would not work was decisive because it was negative!

In the case of a successful run through the model of the equipment, could he conclude that the process would work under real plant conditions? He would probably refrain from giving an opinion until he had cleared all the discrepancies between the actual plant process and the laboratory-model process by bringing back to a presently observable stage all other features of the actual plant conditions.

Verification and the audit of the future. "The auditor cannot attach his opinion to events of the future because future events are inherently uncertain. Future events escape the control of management and the auditor; therefore, the auditor is not in a position to express an opinion on statements about the future (as, for example, a budget) unless the opinion is negative." In professional circles I have come across the preceding statements, expressed in more or less similar terms, more than once. The essence of the statement is that the auditor's opinion has to be definite and vigorous; therefore, if there is no perceivable past or present evidence, there should not be a positive, affirmative judgment (opinion) on the validity or truth of a proposition.

We have to agree with the above statement as far as it concerns a verification process. Verification is an audit of past or concurrent evidence. However, we understand the concept of audit in a broader sense. In this broader sense the audit includes the evaluation of future evidence. We maintained that the audit of future evidence (an intended or expected evidence) is an investigation process. "Investigation" means the establishment of missing evidence with the help of available surrogates.

It is interesting to note that the most conservative and cautious professional group, public accountants, is actually auditing the future in verifying the financial statements of a corporation; and the public accountants are not only auditing the future, they are also including their findings in an unqualified audit opinion, suggesting the certainty of the future event.

I quote an article from Toronto's *Globe and Mail*:

WASHINGTON. At least four U.S. computer firms have

switched accountants rather than face qualified opinions on a single issue in their annual reports, documents at the Securities and Exchange Commision show.

The switching of accountants—away from such old-line conservative firms as Arthur Andersen and Co. and Price Waterhouse and Co.—was done after the accountants indicated there were uncertainties as to whether revenues from computer rentals would allow the companies to fully recover their investments.

The cause of the dispute was the availability from International Business Machines Corp. of its new system 370 computers. The four companies had IBM 360 computers, and there was concern that customers would rather lease computer services from firms having the newer machines.

The switch is significant in that a corporation's outside auditing firm, according to SEC chairman William J. Casey, "is the only independent public representative immediately involved in the reporting process with the ability to take timely action . . . to protect both management and investors from misleading reports."

The question is whether a corporation that shops around for an accountant in agreement with its version of proper accounting is serving the interests of its shareholders. The SEC is looking into the question.

In the computer line, Boothe Computer Corp. of San Francisco, a large leasing firm with about $60-million in sales last year, and Management Data Corp. of Philadelphia, both switched from Arthur Andersen to Touche Ross and Co.

The reason seems clear: Andersen would have placed a footnote in the annual report to the effect that it was certifying the fairness of the financial statement only subject to the effect of certain future events that could not then be determined.

Touche Ross told Boothe it would not have to issue such a disclaimer.

Two other firms, Banister Continental Corp. of Jenkintown, Pa., and DCL Inc. of Saddle Brook, N.J., also switched accounts this year for precisely the same reason. In both cases the switch was from Price Waterhouse, whose views on whether the firms can successfully recoup their investments in IBM 360 equipment were the same as those of Arthur Andersen.

Banister hired Arthur Young and Co. and DCL retained Lybrand, Ross Bros. and Montgomery.

The four computer companies are among 17 corporations that the SEC staff tentatively believes switched accountants because of differences about how certain transactions should be accounted for.

The outcome could, of course, vastly affect a corporation's earnings report, depending on how the resulting accounting principles are applied.[3]

I have quoted the above article to show that in an audit of a clearly historical (retrospective) nature—such as the audit by the shareholders auditor of a corporation—the audit of the future, the audit of the findings of an investigation (or a guess?), plays an important role.

Yet, in actual practice the most conservative practitioners do state that the *financial statements fairly represent the financial position of a firm at a certain date and the results of the operation for a certain period*. The financial statements themselves are prepared on the assumptions that:

1. The firm will survive (going concern).

2. Assets will collect the cost at which they are recorded (lower of cost or market, conservatism).

3. Depreciation charges are sufficient and not exorbitant to allow the write-off of the costs within a time period in the future.

4. Amortization charges are properly allotted between past, present, and future periods.

The article that I quoted described the consequences of differences in judgment over a future event: the effect on the sales by some companies of a new computer system.

In the opinion of Arthur Andersen and Co., the depreciation charges to write off the fixed-asset cost of certain computer

---

[3] *Toronto Globe and Mail* (Oct. 6, 1972), p. B-3.

installations were not sufficient. Touche Ross and Co. was of the opinion that the depreciation charges are and will be sufficient.

The evidence to support either of the opinions or judgments is a future one. When the time comes, we shall be able to perceive the future principal more closely and decide who were right and who were wrong.

For the tentative establishment of the future principal, we need some surrogates. The future principal: A situation in the future when total accumulated charges and disposal proceeds will more or less equal the costs of the computer installations. Present surrogates: The assertion of management.

The auditors had to search for additional surrogates. Those additional surrogates might have been:

(a) The opinions of other experts in the computer service/sales business.

(b) Their own past experiences in situations similar to the given case. (The validity of those indirect surrogates can be established only by inference.)

(c) Data about the potential of the new series of computers. (The new series affects only the operating unit and not the software, the attachments, and trained personnel. What are the costs of service and service potential with the new series?)

(d) Data about the state of the market. (When could a competitor break into the market with the new unit? Are there any long-term service contracts? What is the value of the expertise gained in dealing with existing clients? Is there any consumer loyalty among the customers?)

Actually the procedure to establish a future principal is an investigation unless the appropriate surrogates are presented to the auditor. If the audited corporation undertook the investigation and if the assertion of future principal is based on a thorough and documented judgment, the auditor is in the position to restrict himself to the last phase of an investigative process: the audit (decision audit).

In this case he will establish the reliability and truth value of the existing surrogates, reconcile them, and then look for clues indicating that the surrogates do not represent the asserted principal. Next he will evaluate the prediction models and decision models available in the situation.

Naturally the auditor can never give an absolute and positive opinion about any future principal. The best he could do would be to state that at present nothing indicates that the future principal will not happen as asserted and expected.

If he finds surrogates of present or future circumstances that conflict with the chain of events necessary for the actualization of the expected future principal, his task is easier. Some surrogates may indicate events that make the arrival of a future principal impossible. This was the case in our example when the auditor observed a chemical process as it was performed by using an exact model of the actual plant. The observed surrogate was the chemical process in the model. The process did not work in the iron-lined tubes and containers. By inference he concluded that the presence of iron instead of glass had an impact on the chemical process in the extraction of alycin from onions; therefore, the process would not work under existing plant conditions. He then was able to come up with a definitive negative opinion: The process will not work under existing plant conditions (a negative outcome of a projection).

If the process had been successful by using the model of the actual plant, could the auditor have asserted that it would also work under actual plant conditions? I doubt it. He could just state: At the moment I know about nothing that would indicate that the process would fail under existing plant conditions.

Therefore, in a future-oriented investigation or audit, the emphasis has to be on clues or surrogates indicating the negative features of the relationship between the assertion (expectations) and the ultimate principal (future event or situation).

Financial statements and hidden assumptions. Predictions or assertions about a future principal are dependent on a multitude of events and circumstances. The number of those events increases with the length of time between the assertion and the date of the principal, the predicted event; the number decreases with the level of effective control that the person making the prediction has over the occurrence of the principal; and it depends on the nature of the component parts of the principal.

In our communication process we are limited by constraints of volume and time. It is impossible to list or mention all the conditions that must be fulfilled in order to render the actualization of the principal a certainty.

Therefore, in every judgment concerning assertions that are about future principals or are partly based on future principals, we have to make some assumptions that are not mentioned. We may call them "hidden" assumptions.

We discussed on the previous pages that after a verification process the shareholders auditor in a corporation gives an opinion on the financial statements presented by the directors. The opinion is usually an affirmative one: "The financial statements represent *fairly* the financial position of the corporation and the results of the operations for the year under review." The financial statements are based on some future value judgments: Receivables will be collected, inventories will be sold, the plant and equipment will be usable in the future and will be disposed of without material losses or profits.

It is clear that the verification process itself does not warrant opinions on those areas. How has the public-accounting profession overcome this problem?

The answer lies in "generally accepted accounting principles." In effect, the auditor's opinion contains the provision "in accordance with generally accepted accounting principles."

As we have seen in Chapter II, the audit performed by the shareholders auditor of a corporation (the statutory audit) consists of two phases. The first phase is that of the verification, the establishment of the truth or reality of the transactions. In this phase the norms (criteria) used to arrive at the interim opinion are those of the "actual reality."

The second phase of the statutory audit consists of the matching of the verified system of surrogates against the norms of the statutory requirements of disclosure "according to generally accepted accounting principles." The financial position of the corporation and the results of its operations are deemed to be expressed "according to generally accepted accounting principles."

Among those principles we find:

1. The principle of "continuity" (going concern). We are assuming that the operations of the firm will continue indefinitely. Receivables will be collected, inventories will be sold, and facilities will be used in the future.

2. The principle of "matching costs and related revenues." Costs that have been incurred and are potentially useful in providing revenues are becoming a part of the "Financial Position Statement" as assets.

3. The principle of "freedom from bias" (objectivity), which requires an unbiased approach to measurements and expectations.

4. The principle of "conservatism," which is in direct conflict with "freedom from bias" and requires that revenues shall be recognized only as they are realized while losses (even future losses) shall be reported as they are recognizable. This principle requires a bias by the auditor in the direction of cautious pessimism: In case of doubt in the future, expect the worst.

5. The principle of "consistency." Be consistent in your methods of measurement and reporting from one year to another.

The above-mentioned principles are incorporated in the norm structure (model of criteria) against which the shareholders auditor is comparing the established, verified evidence model, reduced to the same level of generalization as is required by the statutory rules of reporting.

In the first phase of the audit, the phase of verification, he has no difficulty in establishing the reality of the finished transactions. He can also verify the existence of the unfinished transactions but not their ultimate outcome; also, he is unable to verify the recovery of outlays made to provide the firm with continuous operating capacity in the future, as, for example, in the case of plant, machinery, and equipment. The principle of continuity and the matching of costs and related revenues allow the showing of those outlays as assets. The measurement of the "unmatched" amount, the net-asset value of those outlays, is a judgment requiring the use of a norm structure established by expectations of the future. The future physical life of the assets, the future costs to maintain their capacity, the effects of technological change on their usableness, and so forth, are not known when the judgment about the expiration of their original cost is made.

Actually, if the shareholders auditor wants to be exact, he should state in his opinion on the financial statements of the client corporation that he tested the completed transactions and the outlays for future transactions. With respect to the recovery of the outlays for future transactions, he cannot have an opinion based on historical facts, and he cannot verify their recovery unless it happened before the date of his opinion. If the recovery is still in the future, he should state his assumptions to the reader in order to prevent misunderstandings in the communication process between himself and the user of his opinion.

THE EVALUATION OF ATTITUDES

We live and work in a society composed of human persons. We receive data from humans; we are exposed to their representations, statements, and judgments. We rely on those representations in arriving at opinions and in deciding how to act or how not to act. On the other hand, our statements, opinions, or judgments, if communicated to others, are used by others for information, decisions, and so forth.

Because of the limited "scope of attention" of the person who is responsible for the final or formal opinion, the audit process itself is usually a group effort. The person responsible relies on representations, on judgments made by members of his audit team, and on surrogates originating from different human sources. These surrogates reach him through the communication process; therefore, we have to construct our entire theory of auditing around the communication process.

On the opposite side of the communication process, we see the other humans, persons just like we are. They are similar to us but are not completely identical. Their goals may be different from ours; their norms for making judgments and statements are unknown to us; their judgment process and their statement mechanization may be faulty, based on hearsay or imaginary evidence. Therefore, we have to know the way of thinking and judging used by persons with whom we are dealing. If we want to rely on their statements or actions in the future, we have to know their "attitudes" (goals), whether they are hidden or openly admitted.

The evaluation of attitudes is an investigation if there is not sufficient evidence available and an evaluation process if we have to confirm or negate a representation about a certain individual.

Perceivable human activities consist of human acts (what somebody did or does) and data from verbal or written communications consisting of statements or opinions or by other perceivable data (signs).

The first step in the process of investigation is to determine the goal or purpose of the investigation. Is it our goal to find out how reliable a statement of the individual is or how he will act in the future? The goal will determine the norm system (criteria) used in our final opinion about the individual.

The next stage in the process is that of expansion. We collect data about the individual: statements he has made, opinions he holds, his actions in the present and in the past.

The opinions, statements, and actions of the individual under investigation have to be analyzed. We have to try to reconstruct by inference the underlying goals, his ambitions. Next we determine whether a representation made by the individual or an action of the individual was the result of a deliberate and logical opinion or whether it was sheer imitation of others, a routine social act. Both appear in the same grammatical form. We cannot consider a statement about the weather as evidence for "sound judgment and reliability" or "truthfulness." Neutral small talk may be indicative of an emotional stage, but it has to be dismissed unless it contains clues showing some areas to be investigated. Therefore, the familiarity with the "context," with the circumstances under which an act was committed or a statement was made, is of primary importance.

Statements, representations, or actions that are considered out of context are not valid surrogates as evidence to be used for a more generalized judgment about an individual. Unfortunately, all individual actions and individual statements are happening in a given time under certain conditions. Ideally it would be desirable to dismiss them and not to rely on them; unfortunately, we have to make future-oriented decisions assuming a certain behavior on the parts of persons around us. Since we have no other indications for the reliability of the individual members of the society, we have to use our past and present experience for the construction of a behavioral model of an individual that will be valid both in the past and in the future.

Usually we construct our model (the "behavioral pattern" of an individual or groups of individuals) by intuition, by "feeling." We may even have a rule of thumb, developed by experience, to measure the attitudes and capacities of an individual or group.

We mentioned that familiarity with goals of the individuals under investigation is useful; it is necessary to have knowledge of the circumstances in which an action took place or a statement was made.

Limitations of time and our own restricted scope of attention, as well as insufficient data on the individuals, are terrible hurdles in the investigation of attitudes. From a few observed acts or a few statements, we have to build possible models of attitudes of past or future behavior for an individual as we arrive in the model-building stage of the investigation.

While discussing the investigation, we mentioned that the multitude of information received falls into separate individual models in the imagination of the investigator, depending on his schemata in the data bank. The data bank comes alive as previous encounters with similar information groups are organized in certain schemata.

We can make the model-building more accurate if we analyze the observed acts and the representations made by an individual or group. We can dissolve an act into its component parts:

1. What was the goal or purpose of the act?
2. What was the decision underlying the act?
3. How was the decision reached?
4. What decision model was used in reaching the decision?
5. What projection model was used to reach the decision?

Decisions and projections are made out of judgments (opinions). Every representation or statement made, every opinion or judgment, is composed of the following conceptual parts:

a. A goal or purpose.
b. A system of norms or criteria which is dependent on the goal.
c. Evidence which is adjusted to the norm system.
d. Judgment proper, the synopsis and connection of the evidence and criteria (norm system).

We may not be able to have enough information to clear up all the component parts of some action. Our task is made easier and simpler by analyzing several statements or opinions.

The center of the investigation of attitudes is always an individual or a group. If we are in the possession of several statements by or judgments of an individual, we can compare the representations by "mapping" them. But first we have to ask: What was the acknowledged and apparent purpose of the statements? Did the apparent or publicized goals conform to the system of norms that was applied? Is there no contradiction between the acknowledged goal and the criteria (norm system) used? What was the evidence available for the person stating the opinion or making the judgment? Is he in the habit of making goal-oriented statements and decisions, or is he simply imitating judgments made by somebody else?

By noting the component parts and eventually putting them on paper, we may map an outline of them. We may find both contradictions and similarities. The personality or the attitudes of the individual or the group may emerge in front of us from the comparison. We may either confirm or discard the apparent or acknowledged goals of the person as a source of information. On the other hand, we may get valuable information about his attitudes for the future. We could better predict his future behavior.

A few days ago I read about a financier who acquired control of a major international company. According to the book written about him, he transferred the valuable assets of the companies controlled by the group through a series of mergers, sales, and spin-offs to dummy companies, dummy banks, and secret numbered accounts.

The acknowledged goal of every director of a corporation and of every member of a government is to act in the interests of the shareholders (the "company") or in the interest of the "people" (country). Naturally we have to admit that every director or public administrator has additional goals; we are not living a "single goal" life! Those goals include power, wealth, maintenance of the position, promotion. As long as those individual or party goals are not in conflict with the acknowledged or publicized goals of the individual or group, they have to be tolerated, as we all are humans. But if, in case of the conflict of goals, the hidden goals determine the criteria (norm system) for decisions or judgments, the directors or public administrators are not living up to the trust placed in them by the shareholders or voters.

The auditor, or the investigator, is not in a position to question the actual goals and criteria used in evaluating single statements or in analyzing single decisions; but if he has possession of several statements or decisions, he can map the inferences that he made from them and come up with a model of actual goals and criteria.

The sale of material and valuable assets to a newly formed company may or may not be an error. The auditor could analyze the decision; determine the decision maker; and analyze the decision as to "acknowledged" goals, criteria, the projection model, and evidence available to the decision maker or judge. Another transaction will follow. The auditor or investigator will do the same. By mapping several decisions (or statements or judgments), we may see a pattern, a model, emerge. The emerging model is showing the "attitude" of the person or group under investigation and evaluation.

We may find that we have several possible models. Which one is the most important for our purpose? The model that is relevant or most closely connected to the behavior that I am interested in. If I want to evaluate a person's reliability as a source of past-oriented surrogates, his attitudes as a bridge player or as a social entertainer are less important than his ability to reject the hearsay-type of imaginary evidence. Although the human person is an integral entity, together with the environment, we have to focus, for practical purposes, on the group of attitudes that is most relevant for us.

After the establishment of possible models of attitude groups (the hypothesis stage), we enter the next phase of the investigation process, that of the "confirmation." We decide on one or two possible models. We have to look now for surrogates, or new evidence, to confirm or validate our selection.

Major transactions, such as loans, mergers, and acquisitions, that are not in the interest of the shareholders or the supposed beneficiaries of an institution have to be noticed, identified, and mapped in an investigation of the attitudes of top management. Changes in key personnel are equally critical. If we analyze the transactions, the changes, and the method of selecting new top personnel, we would have to outline each transaction and decision, as we mentioned above. We may find that the transactions and decisions indicate goals that conflict with the supposed goals of the organization. For example, we may come up with five possible models of attitudes for the person in control of the organization:

1. A personal-power seeker who is attempting to strengthen his position.
2. A seeker of wealth for personal purposes.
3. A person working in the interest of a third party (a political party, a competitor, etc.).
4. An ignorant person who is misled by false expectations.
5. A genius who expects something or knows something that we do not know.

We may opt for 5 as a probable model. We cannot accept it without additional surrogates or pieces of evidence that confirm our hypothesis. If no immediate judgment is needed, we can wait and see. If we have no time to wait for new future acts, decisions, or representations, we can look for surrogates that contradict hypotheses 1, 2, 3, and 4. We may ask questions; we may generate new representations from the person or group under investigation. The new representations have to be analyzed and the results have to be used to adjust our hypothesis. They may contradict model 5, and then we could adjust our tentative model.

The last stage of the investigation is the audit of our opinion: What was the purpose of our investigation? Is our selected norm system (criteria) applicable in the given situation? Do we have enough evidence to warrant an opinion on the attitudes of a person or a group? Who will use our opinion if we arrived at one? How shall we communicate our opinion?

Although the investigation of attitudes has its foundations in acts, decisions, and representations made in the immediate or remote past, our opinions or judgments will be used by us or others for future decisions and eventually for actions. For that reason we must use our findings carefully. The most relevant for our purposes are the attitudes prevailing in the future, when we expect an action, decision, or reaction from the person or group of persons whose past or present attitudes we have investigated.

What influences will or may change those attitudes until the critical moment comes? We can change attitudes "at gunpoint," with pressure, control (education), persuasion, and so forth. We are again in the area of predicting the future, in "planning." So we have no final solution. We can only improve our approach and be intellectually better prepared to deal with the present sources of the future events.

CHAPTER VIII
THE PRINCIPLES OF AUDITING

IN *The American Heritage Dictionary of the English Language*, we find the following definitions for the expression "principle" (noun):

> 1. A basic truth, law, or assumption. 2.a. A rule or standard, especially of good behavior. 2.b. Moral or ethical standards or judgments collectively. 3. A fixed or predetermined policy or mode of action. 4. A basic, or essential, quality or element determining intrinsic nature or characteristic behavior. 5. A rule or law concerning the functioning of natural phenomena or mechanical processes. 6. A basic source. 7. *Capital* P. *Christian Science*. God.[1]

As we see, the usage of the term "principle" is rather loose. It can be used to mean "postulates" (1), "attitudes" (2 and 3), and even "God" (7). We will use it in the meaning of 5 as an essential quality or element determining the intrinsic nature of a "good" audit.

We may adhere to certain principles, or we may not follow those principles. We may be auditing, judging, or arriving at opinions without following the principles; and our action will still be audit, judgment, or opinion. But by following the principles recommending a certain type of action and behavior, our chances for errors in our audits, judgments, or opinions will be lower and the quality of the resulting audits will be better. Inherent in the idea of "principle" is that "principles" are at a higher level of generalization. One meaning of the word "principle" (6) is "a basic source." In this meaning we could call this book on *Theory of Auditing* the *Principles of Auditing Theory*.

[1] *The American Heritage Dictionary of the English Language*, ed. W. Morris (New York: American Heritage Publishing Co., 1969), s.v. "principle."

I remember reading a book which was supposed to be about generally accepted accounting principles, in which I could not find any generalizations at a higher level. It simply described present practices at a transaction treatment level without any attempt to explain the treatment with reference to more general principles, as, for example, the "Matching Principle," the "Realization Principle," and so forth. The author evidently used the term "principle" as in meaning 6, intending to present the book as a basic source of presently accepted accounting treatments of the usually encountered transactions.

We will use the term "principle" differently. Our principles are a group of guidelines or recommendations to be followed in auditing practice if we want a good audit, a correct opinion or judgment.

Naturally the listing and discussion is not exhaustive. We have to ignore the elementary requirements (for example, that the auditor shall be able to read and write and understand the language in which the surrogates are presented). We are also limited in the listing and discussion of the principles by the "law of diminishing attention," by the reader's expected scope of attention. Too many principles would tend to water down the attention that the more important ones deserve.

THE PRINCIPLE OF EXCLUSIVENESS

Every audit has to have a purpose. The purpose of the audit determines the judgment (opinion), the norms to be applied, and the evidence to be used. An audit cannot exist if it has no purpose; and it cannot be good or efficient if it has no well-defined purpose or if it tries to serve several purposes.

Let us recall the audit executed by my mother when I refused to accept her conclusion that there were mice in her bedroom. The purpose of her audit was to determine the presence of mice. She elected to use our cat as a tool of the audit, and she observed the behavior of the cat at the spot where the noises (the surrogates) originated. Would her selection of the cat make sense if she had had as a purpose the elimination of the noises? If we had decided to eliminate the noises, the whole audit would have taken a different direction.

Our second example discussed was that of the audit performed by a judge in a criminal case. He had as his purpose the enforcement of the Criminal Code. He achieved his purpose by (a) establishing the evidence, an activity geared to ascertain retroactively a chain of events as past or historical reality; (b) comparing the acts of a person or several persons to the categories set out in the Criminal Code; and (c) arriving at a conclusion (the judgment).

If the judge had other purposes beyond the enforcement of law in each individual case, his audit would have been incorrect. If his purpose had been to enforce the law and to seek political or other favors, could he have performed his audit correctly? I just read in the newspapers about two mistrials by a judge who, in his honest effort to fight crime, convicted persons on insufficient evidence. He extended the concept of his purpose; he did not adhere to it; and his judgments proved to be incorrect.

The importance of our principle is perhaps more prevalent, if that is possible, in the case of a group audit. The individual members of the group have to have a well-defined idea of the purpose of the audit in order to evaluate the importance of clues in order to limit or extend the procedures used and to focus their attention on the fringe areas in observing the details of evidence. They have to know the extent of information channeled to other members of the group.

The lack of application of the principle of the unity of purpose resulted in an interesting dilemma and an uncertain situation for the shareholders auditors in North America in the second half of the sixties. The institution of the "shareholders audit by an independent accountant" originated in England in 1844. The shareholders of a corporation have access to certain records of their corporation but not to the books in which the daily operations, other than those connected with the issue and transfer of shares, are recorded and summarized. The partners in a partnership have access to all records. The problem was how to provide the shareholders with reliable information about the state of the business. The answer was found by requiring the directors of the corporation to publish financial statements and make them available to shareholders on record. But how can the shareholders be sure that the financial statements are in accordance with the books and records of the corporation and that the reported results of the operations are correct? The shareholders have no right of access to the records that serve as sources for the statements.

The solution was the institution of the audit by the shareholders auditor, an expert accountant. The auditor, as a trustee of the shareholders, received the right of access to all records of the corporation; he had the right to ask questions of the management, and he had the duty to report on the financial statements presented to the shareholders. In this framework the purpose of the audit was to ascertain that proper books and records were kept by the directors, that the financial statements were in accordance with the records of the corporation, and that the profit or loss was correctly determined and reported. The shareholders auditor received adequate rights to gather the necessary evidence for this purpose.

With the passage of time the original purpose of the audit by an expert accountant, which consisted of assuring that the shareholders receive reliable information from records to which they had no access, was forgotten; and the auditor had to note, in his report on the financial statements, whether they represented a true, fair, or correct picture of the corporation's financial position and operations.

The purpose of the audit was extended. The original audit procedures—the checking of records to ascertain proper recording, consistent cut-off procedures, and inspection of source documents—were adequate for the purpose of an opinion on the relationship of the corporate business records and the financial statements, but they were inadequate for the extended purpose.

We could illustrate the 19th-century audit of the shareholders auditor in Figure 18.

The shareholders auditor moved along lines with the information pyramid that were available within the corporation. He relied on internally originated surrogates. He had no rights, and he needed no right, to move out from this pyramid.

As the additional purpose of reporting—namely, the fair, true, or correct presentation of the financial position by the financial statements—was added, the evidence provided by the internal information pyramid of the corporation became insufficient. The "financial position" means a relationship to the outside world, to information provided by other than inside sources. The present

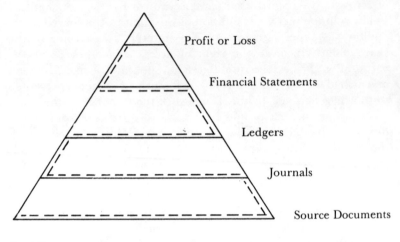

Figure 18

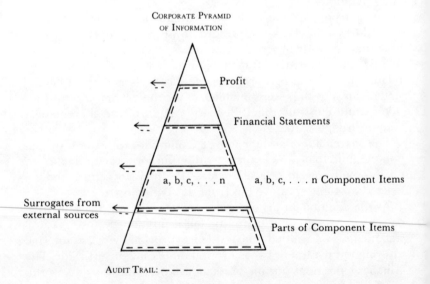

Figure 19

values, the anticipated proceeds of items recorded at cost, are needed for an opinion on the financial position. But the shareholders auditor had no right to obtain information or evidence from outside sources; his only legal instrument for obtaining it was to ask management to provide it for him.

The desired audit procedures could be illustrated in Figure 19.

The audit trail leads to the parts that make up the component items of the financial statements, but the audit trail has to leave the formal information pyramid of the firm.

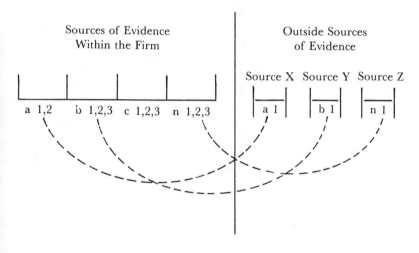

Figure 20

The audit trail has to go outside the pyramid presented by the records of the firm (internal evidence), and it has to establish the validity of the individual items with reference to outside information which is not available within the firm.

Working only within the information pyramid of the firm would violate the "stereo principle" of reliable evidence (see p. 208) and to move outside the pyramid is impossible because the existing statutes regulating the corporations give no rights for doing so. The professional associations, in their recommendations, devised a compromise: The auditor has to ask management to require the outside parties, who are in possession of the necessary evidence, to confirm the items in question for the auditor. But if the management of the corporation refuses to cooperate, the auditor can only deny an opinion or qualify his opinion. Management is under no legal duty to ask the outside parties for evidence, and the outside parties have no obligations to provide it.

So, shareholders auditors are in a quandary. In a series of legal decisions in the United States from 1962 to 1970, they were held responsible to parties other than shareholders of the corporation for the existence or collectibility of assets and for valuation of investments, although their report was addressed to the shareholders and their methods of obtaining evidence were restricted by legislation. It is clear that their audit is not adequate to satisfy the extended purpose, as it was devised for the more restricted one: namely, to give an opinion on the relationship of financial statements to the information recorded in the books of account and the documents of the corporation to the shareholders who have no access to those sources.

THE PRINCIPLES OF NORMS

The principles grouped around the concept of norms (criteria) in the audit activity deal with the quality or possible quality of the audit in relationship to the norms or system of norms against which the evidence is compared in the judgment.

They consist of:

1. The principle of unity (consistency) of norms.
2. The principle of objectivity of norms.
3. The principle of relevance (pertinence) of norms.

UNITY OF NORMS

Throughout the audit process the auditor has to use a well-defined and unchangeable set of norms.

The norms against which the evidence will be compared in the judgment have to be defined and understood by the judge or auditor. The auditor's opinion, or judgment, will be used by the auditor or by other persons. In the retrospective (or historical) audit the usual norm is: Was the event or series of events, which were defined by the purpose of the audit, true (existing) or not? The most common norm is that of validity, reality, or truth (verification). The selection of evidence, the audit trail, has to be decided on by the auditor; otherwise he would be lost in the unrelated mass of data, which would evoke unrelated schemata in the imagination of the auditor. I want to establish the reality of the data resulting in the perception of a sentence provided by my hearing "You are a great man." I see a man sitting in front of me, and I remember the movement of his lips as he pronounced the sounds making up the sentence. I accept the sentence as valid data. I use an additional (stereo) surrogate provided by another organ of mine—my sight. If I had not seen his lips moving, I might have asked him, "What did you say?"

But if I am not interested in the validity of the source data but in the validity of the statement, content, or interpretation of the data, I will not ask him if he said it or not. I may simply evoke some schemata related to my opinion about myself (past surrogate) and conclude that I am really a great man; therefore, the sentence is true, and because the statement is true, the data were real. I switched from the norm of validity (or existence) of data to the norm of validity of content. The switching of norms is a usual source of errors and misconceptions.

In our example of the anticipatory (future) audit, we analyzed the audit of the feasibility of producing alycin from onions under existing conditions in a chemical plant. The norm applied was feasibility in the given plant. If during the audit process the machinery in the plant were changed, the result of the audit would certainly be incorrect and irrelevant, and the audit effort would be unnecessary.

The importance of the principle of unity of norms is even more evident if we consider the audits performed by groups. The norms to be applied to satisfy the purpose of the audit have to be understood and used by each member of the group. They will consider the surrogates (the eventual clues) in the light of the norms. An uncommunicated change or switch in the norms would create an anarchy of methods, a disorder, resulting in useless waste of effort and time. If the switch in norms were to go unnoticed, the results would culminate in a disastrous audit opinion or judgment.

Changes in the application of the norms may originate from unawareness of the norms, from sheer ignorance, or from the attitude of the person applying them. The uniform and consistent application of norms is called objectivity in the audit.

Objectivity requires disciplined thinking, awareness of the norms to be applied, moral strength, and fortitude. The concept of objectivity is related not only to the application of the norms but also to the consistency of the norms themselves.

OBJECTIVITY OF NORMS

Norms applied in a judgment have to be objective. *Objectivity* is defined as "1. The state, condition, or quality of being objective" and "2. External or material reality." For our purpose we can forget for a moment meaning 2, but we have to inquire further into the meaning of the term "objective." Objective (as an adjective) means: "1. Of or having to do with a material object as distinguished from a mental concept, idea, or belief. (Compare 'subjective.') 2. Having actual existence or reality. 3.a. Uninfluenced by emotion, surmise, or personal prejudice. b. Based on observable phenomena; presented factually (*an objective appraisal*)." Meanings 4 and 5 are medical and grammatical, so we disregard them; meaning 6 is "Serving as a goal; being the object of a course of action (*an objective point*)."[2]

In the different meanings of the adjective "objective," we can discover three different levels of "objectivity." The first level, according to meaning 1 of the term, would be adherence to the material, tangible point of external data (low level of generalization). The personal, subjective element of the world would be excluded from this level of the concept.

This interpretation of the concept is usable or valid only for Robinson Crusoe, living in isolation. But even Robinson had his memories of the human society, of himself, of living creatures, persons, or emotions, experiences of his own. The schemata (the parts of the human memory in which our surviving informations are stored) do not distinguish between material objects and immaterial ones. Material objects become immaterial as we form concepts from the data perceived about them.

[2] *American Heritage Dictionary,* s.v.v. "objectivity," "objective."

As human beings we are living in a society; we are members of different groups—family, friends, and so forth. In our communication with other members of the groups, we have to accept certain representations of others. Our intellectual ability to create and store information exceeds by far the data-perceiving limits of our senses. The human animal is plagued by his overgrown fantasy. The phenomenon of accepting representations or opinions provided by others as truth or reality is the origin of collective actions, collective opinions, and group behavior. Almost all of our knowledge, our opinion of the world or even of ourselves, is simply taken over from other human beings without being verified against the norm of reality. This type of memory is inherently no different in an individual from the memory created by firsthand perceptions.

If I don't believe my eyes and therefore ignore the data provided by my eyes indicating the presence of a table in front of me, I will be punished: I will bump against the table.

If I don't believe what the textbooks and teachers have told me and therefore don't answer the questions on examinations as they require it, I fail in my course. I get punished. We conclude that the existence of certain things, relationships, and judgments is determined by the effects of belief (acceptance) or nonbelief (nonacceptance) in them. From our childhood on, we learn by experience that it is better to be on the cautious side and accept the beliefs of our group, especially if a verification of the realities underlying the beliefs is beyond our means and capacities.

Under closer scrutiny of the term "objective," meaning 1 disappears as being too narrow and untrue. It melts into meaning 2 ("having actual existence or reality") as a general term applied to everything having a potential effect on the surrounding world or on ourselves. "Material" and "immaterial" are only classifications that could be useful in the description of certain phenomena. So we shall modify the meaning of the first level of objectivity by switching from meaning 1 of the concept to meaning 2: The first level of objectivity, then, is *adherence to actual existence or reality and not only material existence or reality.*

How shall we interpret the principle of objectivity of norms at the first level of objectivity? At this level, the principle requires that the norms shall be existing norms. In the case of the basic audit (verification of the audit for the reality of data), the norms are those of the actual existence assumed as a cause from perceiving the effects of the data. Did it happen? Was it true?

In other types of audits the norms have different types of existence. The law exists as a system of norms because it is accepted by a group of human beings, and it has an effect. The reality of the law can be proven by its effects. In addition, it is recognizable from its sources—the statutes and the common law.

The judge who applied nonexisting law would come up with an incorrect judgment. An operational auditor who applied as norms for his opinion not the policy and goals set by management but norms set by a group aiming to gain rapid promotion or to acquire more power would evidently perform an incorrect audit, and his judgment in his report would be incorrect.

The second level of objectivity has its roots in meaning 3a and 3b of the term "objective." It means *freedom from emotion, surmise, or personal prejudice.* The principle of objectivity of norms at this level requires from the auditor a continuous effort to suppress schemata that interfere with the absolute and quasi-mechanical interpretation of the norms. It is very hard to suppress sympathies, preferences, and emotions that are inherent in a human being. The human person is enslaved by the big goal of his existence: the continuous expansion of the human race, of his individual race, nation, family, religious group, and so forth. Moral convictions and prejudices arising from education and experience are realities that cannot be denied.

An audit involves persons. The auditor's attitude to the persons who have an interest in the opinion or judgment will always influence the interpretation of the norms and the selection of the norms that are applied. A male jury will always be more lenient to a pretty woman than to another man. We can understand the sympathies or antipathies, but we have to realize that they endanger the quality of the audit. The purpose of the audit and the prevailing social opinion will determine the acceptable tolerance in the application of the principle of objectivity at our second level. Sometimes we use programmed precaution to prevent bias in the interpretation of norms: Examination papers do not show the names of the candidates. The examiner tries to avoid data and information that might cause potential bias and lack of objectivity in the interpretation of norms in forming an opinion on the papers submitted.

We cannot require from an auditor that he shall deny his human nature; we can only ask him to try to restrain his subjectivity and to remain within acceptable limits, within the limits of tolerance in the interpretation of the norms.

A third level of objectivity is related to meaning 6 of the term: "serving as a goal, being the object of a course of action." Norms serve the goal if they are relevant to the purpose of the audit. If they are irrelevant, the resulting audit or judgment will be useless and incorrect for the purpose to be served.

With this sense of the term "objective" at the third level of objectivity, we arrive at the principle of relevance (pertinence) of norms. I preferred to differentiate between the principle of objectivity of norms and the principle of relevance of norms for the sake of clarity of presentation. It is difficult to have in mind all three levels of objectivity (existence, interpretation, and relevance) and to explain always which level we have in mind when we refer to it. It is simpler and less misleading to separate at least the third level of objectivity and treat it as a different principle—the principle of relevance.

RELEVANCE OF NORMS

The principle of relevance of norms asserts that the norms applied in the judgment or opinion have to be relevant, or pertinent, to the purpose of the audit. It points out the relationship between the purpose to be served by the audit and the selection of norms (criteria) to be applied. Application of norms that are not relevant to the purpose will result in an incorrect audit.

If the purpose of the audit is to give an opinion to a potential buyer of a business on the price that he should pay for it, the norms to be applied are present market price on a liquidation basis or on a going-concern replacement basis. If the purpose of the audit is to give an opinion to the shareholders of the same business on the fairness of the financial statements, the norms to be applied are historical retrospective truth and proper disclosure. The mixing of the two norms would create incorrect opinions and incorrect audits.

But how do we know what is relevant or pertinent? Who tells us what is relevant? What is the meaning of the term "relevance"? Relevance is "the state or quality of being relevant." "Relevant" (adjective) means "related to the matter at hand; to the point; pertinent."[3] Relevance is therefore a relationship between two concepts. One is the "matter at hand," the purpose, the problem. The other is an event, a thing, or a norm, as in our problem under discussion.

In this sense, relevance expresses the relationship that is implied by meaning 6 of "objective": "serving as a goal; being the object of a course of action."

The purpose of an opinion is the object of the course of action. The course of action presupposes a decision based on a decision model, prediction models, and data available. The audit provides assurance that (1) action is taken, if necessary (attention-directing), (2) data available are reliable (verification), or (3) the decision and prediction models are not incorrect. The assurance usually consists of the clarification of one or more attributes of a data group (the objects of a representation).

The norms have to serve the purpose of the judgment or opinion. Unless this is so, the audit is incorrect. The same relationship is expressed by the term "relevance." The difference is only in the emphasis. In the term "relevance," the emphasis (the starting point) is on the concept "serving the purpose." In the term "objective" (meaning "serving as a goal"), the emphasis is on the purpose, on the goal of the audit. But both terms imply a relationship, and the relationship is the same.

The concept of relevance. Relevance is a judgment, an opinion on the relationship of a concept, an event, or a phenomenon to a purpose or to a conclusion. Let us analyze the concept of relevance. The purpose of our inquiry is to establish the nature of relevance. The norm to be applied is that of truth or reality. Is relevance true or not?

The next problem is that of the evidence. Our evidence is the actual use of the term. We read about relevant costs, relevant evidence, relevant norms, and relevant information. What is the

---

[3] *Ibid.,* s.v. "relevance," "relevant."

difference between relevant and irrelevant costs, facts, evidence, or norms?

Something in itself is neither relevant nor irrelevant. As relevance is an opinion, it implies the existence of a conclusion or a purpose. Therefore, relevance exists only if a conclusion or a purpose exists. Without the conclusion or purpose, the concept of relevance is not existent; it is meaningless. Without knowing the conclusion, we cannot know the relevance of anything.

If we use the term "relevance" before knowing the conclusion or the mental process of the comparison or the measurement resulting in the judgment, we are either using a meaningless term or we are anticipating the process and the results of the final conclusion.

We cannot assume that lawyers, auditors, and analysts who are using the term are acting against logic by using the term. They have to anticipate the conclusion or opinion by using it. And if a conclusion has not yet been reached or if an opinion has not yet been formed by the trier (the judge), they not only anticipate the conclusion but, by using the adjective "relevant," they suggest a particular conclusion. The facts, evidence, and norms that are earmarked by the user as relevant before he knows a conclusion show the existence of a preconceived final conclusion in the mind of the persons using the adjective. The term "relevant" has a suggestive value and not real empirical existence if it is used before the final conclusion or judgment is made. The person using it suggests that the judge, auditor, or trier will use the evidence, facts, or phenomenon for his judgment. He could say just as well, "If you will not base your final conclusion on the phenomena (surrogates) presented by me as relevant, your judgment will be incorrect."

The anticipatory use of the term "relevant," or "anticipatory relevance," has, therefore, suggestive purposes. In the anticipatory sense, relevance has no empirical real existence.

Relevance can be established only after a conclusion or judgment is made. Before the determination of the relationship between judgment, norms, and evidence used for the judgment, relevance simply does not exist. Therefore, we cannot have an opinion on their relationship. If we anticipate one of the concepts, we have to anticipate the relationship; but after the existence and definition of both concepts, their relationship can be determined.

We can establish relevance after the conclusion or judgment has been stated. Relevant will be all the information having an effect on the conclusion or judgment. In order to find out the information that has an effect on the conclusion, judgment, or decision, we have to analyze it. Only by subsequent analysis can we find out whether an information was relevant or not. So, relevance exists only in retrospect. It is a retroactive opinion on the information. In this sense it can be established empirically, and it has "real" existence. If I know a decision and, even more, if I am aware of the mental processes of the decision maker in arriving at his conclusion, I can point out the relevant norms (criteria) and the relevant information (evidence) used in arriving at the conclusion. We may conclude that suggestive or anticipatory relevance has no real existence. It is only an instrument of persuasion; but retrospective relevance has an empirical real existence.

We cannot deny the importance of anticipatory relevance although it has no empirical real existence. It has importance in the mental process of the judge. The person making a judgment or conclusion revises in his memory the different schemata stored in his memory. He may recall schemata evoked by various perceptions linked by apprehensible or inapprehensible ties. He will make a conscious effort both to lock out from the conscious field of his present memory anything that is obviously irrelevant and to reduce the content of this conscious present memory to schemata having potential relevance. Potential relevance is a relative term. It usually depends on the experience of the person who is seeking the opinion or solution to a problem. Experience, the scope of the imagination, and knowledge of surrounding circumstances will have an effect on what the trier or decision maker will consider to be potentially relevant. Potential relevance is a type of anticipatory relevance. It has only potential existence; it may or may not become "real," empirically existing, if the trier or decision maker is using the evidence for his actual conclusion.

Validity, objectivity, and relevance. In connection with objectivity and relevance, we have to discuss another term used sometimes as synonymous to objectivity or relevance. The term is "validity."

Validity means "the state or quality of being valid." Valid can mean "1. Well-grounded; sound; supportable: . . . 2. Producing the desired results; efficacious: . . . 3. Legally sound and effective; incontestable, binding: . . . 4. *Logic:* a. Containing premises from which the conclusion may logically be derived: *a valid argument.* b. Correctly inferred or deduced from a premise: *a valid conclusion.* . . .[4]

Something is well-grounded or supportable if it is objective in the sense of the first level of objectivity. The meaning extends beyond the first level of objectivity and reaches over into the second level (without bias) and third level (serving a goal). It overlaps with relevant, as something that is "supportable or sound" may be relevant. I chose the latter terms only because they are used often in the literature, and I have preferred not to use different terms for the sake of "putting old wine in new bottles." Meaning 2 of the adjective "valid" ("producing the desired results") denotes "objectivity at the third level" (serving as an object, a purpose) and also "relevant." If anything produces the desired results, it serves a purpose. We can disregard the legal meaning of the term "valid" for the moment.

Meaning 4a ("containing premises from which the conclusion may logically be derived") is almost identical with "relevant." The slight difference lies in the connotation of the "logically be derived" part of the meaning. It assumes logically correct procedures. I chose the term "relevant" in discussion of the premises.

However, I shall use the term "valid" in the sense of 4b ("correctly inferred or deduced from a premise: *a valid conclusion*") in dealing with one of the principles of judgment, the validity of judgment. In this meaning, "valid" is conclusion- or judgment-oriented, while relevant is premise-oriented. Therefore, it seems appropriate to use "relevance" when discussing the principle of relevance of norms (as criteria are premises for the judgment or opinion) and "validity" when discussing the principle of validity of judgment (because judgment is a conclusion and validity is conclusion-oriented).

THE PRINCIPLES OF JUDGMENT

The discussion of the terms "objective," "relevant," and "valid" bring us to the principles that are grouped around the judgment,

---

[4] *Ibid.*, s.vv. "validity," "valid."

opinion, or conclusion. The five principles of judgment are:

1. The principle of validity (existence) of the judgment.
2. The principle of competence of the judge.
3. The principle of independence of the judge.
4. The principle of completeness of the judgment.
5. The principle of communicability of the judgment.

VALIDITY OF THE JUDGMENT

The principle of validity of judgment deals with the relationship between the norms to be applied and the evidence as shown by the judgment or opinion. The norms to be applied and the evidence are the premises. Their relationship has to be evaluated in the process of synopsis (comparison), and the conclusion will be the judgment or opinion. The principle indicates that a proper synopsis, a comparison of the norms (criteria) and the evidence, should be made and that judgments (opinions) should not be rendered without doing this.

If I repeat a statement without being aware of the criteria (norms) or without having any evidence, I am violating the principle of validity (existence) of the judgment. I may repeat statements that I have read in newspapers, or I may repeat gossip ("facts" that I know nothing about). I may present my opinion or statement because it fits my emotional state or because it may promote my purposes. It may be that the opinions or judgments are even correct, but I did not know their truth. I could not substantiate or prove my representation or judgment.

Unfortunately, only a few of the professionals are aware of the strict logical structure of the judgment. We can only hope that they will know more about it in the future.

We face difficulties with the "general purpose" statements. They are presented in our social communications in the same grammatical form as the judgments but without a careful synopsis of the evidence and the norm system (criteria). We have to rely on the interpretation of the circumstances in separating valid judgments from gossip and hearsay statements.

COMPETENCE OF THE JUDGE

In the previous sections we dealt with the difficulties that the person arriving at an opinion or judgment encounters in making the judgment. Complete awareness and detailed knowledge of the norms to be applied, as well as ability to concentrate and think logically, are required in order to make a correct judgment. In addition, the evidence has to be tested, transformed to the generalization level of the criteria (norm system), and then accepted. We can expect the required qualities only from persons who are well-versed in the areas of reality in which the judgment has to be made and who are, in addition, aware of the intricacies and all the categories of the norms to be applied. An ignorant person may come up with valid and purpose-oriented judgments by sheer intuition or by imitation, but the probability is slight that his judgment will be valid if he is left alone in a new situation.

This requirement is expressed by the principle of competence of the judge. Every opinion is as good as the person forming it and as good as the information available for him to use in forming the opinion.

Competence is the state or quality of being competent, and "competent" means "1. Properly or well qualified; capable. 2. Adequate for the purpose; suitable; sufficient. . . ."[5]

Both meanings are similar. Applied to the person making the judgment, they denote a person who has the knowledge, experience, and ability to select the proper norms, apply them correctly to the well-chosen evidence, and come up with a good or valid judgment.

Competence is a question of opinion. There is no absolute yardstick for measuring it. An individual may be competent, and his judgments may be correct; but competence that is not recognized as such by the persons who have to rely on it has no social effect. Competence has double implications. The first one refers to the internal quality of the person making the judgment. The second refers to the belief or trust in the competence of the judge by anybody who accepts the judgment and thereby renders it socially effective.

In order to ensure competence, professional bodies were organized. Formal training requirements, experience, and examinations ensure that in important sectors of the society the "professional expert" who is the "professional source" of opinions in his field will possess the required knowledge and experience. Degrees, titles,

---

[5] *Ibid.*, s.v. "competent."

and denominations indicate to the public the competence of the organized professionals in their field.

Can we evaluate, or audit, the competence of a person? It is an intriguing task, and it is possible to do this if we have the opportunity to observe him in different judgment situations. We dealt with this problem under "Investigation of Attitudes." We must have evidence for our audit, or we must create it by investigation. The evidence consists of several judgment situations. To avoid the error of taking a "judgment by imitation" as evidence, it is necessary to observe judgments made in various situations of life.

A person cannot be a good judge on the bench or a good shareholders auditor and meanwhile be a careless driver. We cannot divide a person's attitudes into business life and home life. The character is one and indivisible. It may change during the lifetime of an individual as he accepts different values and relinquishes some held previously.

Members of professions requiring formal judgments, such as doctors, lawyers, judges, and auditors, develop some common characteristics. Sometimes they pose unexpected and seemingly irrelevant questions in order to test a judgment or a piece of evidence. Sometimes they repeat questions in different times and different contexts. They follow the rules of obtaining evidence about the information presented by approaching it from different angles. They are trying to fit the new information into the mental model that they have created from earlier data.

The impact of the principle of competence is even more important in group audits. Group audits can be organized differently. They may be centralized or decentralized.

In the centralized group audit the judgment or final opinion is given by one person who uses the other members of the group for collecting the necessary information to enable him to create the mental image of the evidence that he needs. The difficulty in this case is that the evaluation of evidence collected is performed at lower levels of the data pyramid by persons who cannot discriminate between clues that may become important or relevant and events that are not their concern. If a person is checking sales invoices and is supposed to check them following a random pattern, he may come across a cancelled invoice. He will note in his report that invoice #501 was cancelled. If the person authorized to cancel the invoice has his signature on invoice #501, no further action is taken. For the person who is looking at the collectibility of Accounts Receivable, however, the cancelled invoice may tell a different story. It may serve him as a clue indicating that a material portion of the Accounts Receivable will not be collected but that the merchandise will be returned. For the person checking the valuation of inventories, it may indicate substandard merchandise in stock.

There is no end to the possibilities to the division of labor or the division of functions. The logical accessories to every division of labor are the equivalent precautions to integrate the information. The establishment of the equivalent precautions is the problem. Sometimes this problem is solved by ignoring it because the persons who are supposed to provide it are not competent enough.

The decentralized judgment poses problems of another type. In this type of audit, part of the evidence is available for everybody who is involved in the audit. In practice we see this type of activity in audits performed by experts of different qualifications, usually in operational auditing, in industry, in government, or in military services. The problem here is the lack of ability of humans to provide to the others all the information that is available to them in making a judgment. Norms that are alien to the purpose interfere with the judgments; evidence remains hidden; clues go undetected. Finally, the conclusion or final judgment is made, although it does not follow the principles of a "good audit." Usually the opinion of the most persuasive or powerful member of the group prevails, and his more or less informed opinion is adopted as the opinion of the audit group.

Group audits are created and exist out of necessity. They are a necessary evil from the point of view of audit theory, and the opinions or judgments generated by them have to be regarded with suspicion. It is not by chance that in the development of legal thinking the opinions of dissenting judges have more impact on the development of legal norms than the judgments made by the majority as a deciding group.

INDEPENDENCE OF THE JUDGE

Closely related to the principle of competence of the judge or the author of an opinion is the principle of independence.

Independence is the state or quality of being independent. The adjective "independent" has several meanings. We have to disregard the social, political, and mathematical meanings of the term. For our purposes it means "free from the influence, guidance, or control of another or others; self-reliant" or "not dependent on or affiliated with a larger or controlling group, system, or the like. . . ."[6]

It is evident that independence is associated with objectivity (at the first and second levels) and with competence. Independence permits the exercise of both objectivity and competence. Objectivity is the relationship of the judge or auditor to the surrounding world of facts, while competence is the relationship to his own abilities and values. Independence is the relationship to the surrounding human groups. Naturally, independence cannot be considered as absolute freedom from influence, guidance, or control.

Every audit is determined by its purpose and the norms to be applied. Every auditor, judge, or decision maker is guided by some formal or informal standards, by the rules of logic, his competence, the facts. Finally, every judgment or opinion is controlled by people or groups who may accept or reject the opinion or judgment by accepting it, relying on it, acting on it, or by not doing so. Independence cannot degenerate into the anarchy of the autism or the autocracy of the judge or auditor.

We had better consider the independence of the auditor, judge, or decision maker with regard to the component elements of the audit. As to the purpose of the audit, it is evident that the purpose for a judgment is set; and the person who is selecting norms, collecting or accepting evidence, and arriving at the decision or opinion cannot act "independently" from the purpose. As to the norms applied, the norms to be applied have to fulfill the requirements set out in the discussion of the principles applicable to the norms. The norms to be applied have to serve the purpose, and they have to be understood by the potential users of the opinion. As to the judgment made, the auditor or judge has to obey the principles set out earlier (objectivity, validity, etc.).

We may say that the judgment cannot be independent from

[6] *Ibid.*, s.v. "independent."

the norms and that the evidence used has to be objective. The principles concentrated around the judgment deal with the internal rules of arriving at a correct judgment or opinion. The independence refers to lack of influence, guidance, or control by outsiders, by other people. Independence is not the mental attitude of the auditor; it is the assurance that his personal, emotional, and material interests will not be affected by others because of his communicating an opinion, judgment, finding, or decision. The mental attitude is objectivity. I can afford to be objective and arrive at the opinion that an act committed by somebody is a fraud. I can follow the principles of objectivity, validity, and so forth, of the judgment. I may be fully competent; I may know very well the norms (criteria) applied; and I may be aware of the evidence. But if a person holds me at gun point, I may not communicate my correct opinion or judgment because I am not independent; I am under his control.

The importance of independence in this sense is best recognized in the judicial system of the state. No judge can be removed from his bench as the consequence of his judgment, and no judge should be, at least under ideal conditions, rewarded for his judgments. The first part of the above requirement is implemented in contemporary democracies; the implementation of the second part is more difficult. In the case of other professional judgments or decisions, the principle of independence is not institutionalized to the same extent. Professional associations and enlightened colleagues may stand up for an auditor or a doctor who is persecuted or hurt for an opinion that is disliked by a powerful individual or group but only after the harm has been done.

It is interesting to observe the hypocrisy of the professional accounting bodies and the security exchange regulations dealing with the problem of independence. They emphasize that the auditor giving an opinion on financial statements and prospectuses shall have no financial interest in the firm audited. Ownership of a share by the auditor, by his wife, by his partner, or by the employer of the auditor disqualifies him from rendering an opinion. But they close their eyes and try not to see the problem of much greater importance: the threat of losing the client if the client dislikes the auditor's opinion. The directors of a corporation are elected by the shareholders, and the directors usually represent the most powerful shareholders. If the shareholders auditor contradicts the wishes of the directors or if an internal auditor contradicts the wishes and intentions of his immediate superior, he will lose his client or his job.

I remember very well the instructions received from the managing partners while I was in public practice: "You can do anything with our clients, but don't lose them." Where was our "independence"? In theory the "professions" should stand behind the auditor, but in reality the competing public accounting firms are only happy to add a new client to their list and additional fees to their revenues. The result is the actual application of Gresham's Law formulated for currencies: The independent auditors who stick to their objective opinion are eliminated and forced out of circulation by the auditors who subordinate their independence to their business interest. It is difficult to come up with a solution because we are living in a human society, and the auditors, with their families, want to survive. But the existing situation could certainly be improved.

The recent legal cases in the United States prove that the shareholders of a corporation are not the only group that relies on the auditor's opinion attached to a financial statement. Creditors, future investors, the government, and, in general, the public are also among the users. But the corporate regulations give the right of control and the right of removing the auditor for the next year to the shareholders and, in actual practice, to the directors, who propose the change in auditors to the shareholders. The shareholders auditor is in a difficult situation: He is controlled by the directors, but he is also responsible to others. He is on a tightrope, trying to keep his position between the power of the managers, directors, and shareholders and the menacing liability to potential and unknown users of the financial statements.

In the ideal situation the shareholders auditor would be appointed by a body that is detached from the directors and shareholders of the corporation, and he would not be removable. But where could we find such a "body"? If not the shareholders, then only the government or a semipolitical body could appoint the auditor of a corporation. The line of dependence would be changed but not abolished. And I hear in my ears the cry, "The shareholders would lose the right to select the man who will have access to confidential information; the auditor will become a dictator; the competition for clients will take the form of competition for political influence." There is an element of truth in those objections. The practical solution at the moment could be to strengthen the auditor's independence by making him less vulnerable to the corporation once he is elected. The name of the auditor elected from a group of qualified individuals should become part of the corporate charter or the letters patent. The change in charter or letters patent requires more formalities—a qualified majority vote—and it is noticed by the authority that supervises corporate affairs. A board, committee, or court (accountants' court) should be responsible for authorizing the change in the charter or letters patent with regard to the appointment of the new auditor and the release of the old one. In every instance, the old auditor and the representative of the directors should be required to disclose under oath the circumstances leading to the proposed change, and the change should be authorized by the board if it is not the consequence of resistance by the directors to disclose properly information required by the auditor or the consequence of proper but unpopular action by the auditor. The same board could determine fees and decide on disputes regarding fees.

The sanction for violating the decisions of the board could be the withdrawal of the charter or letters patent and the disqualification of directors from holding corporate positions as directors in the future.

But impending threats of loss of revenues are just one side of the coin. An auditor could be influenced by groups or persons who are interested in the audit or decision and who offer higher fees and additional opportunities for earnings (for example, by engagement as management consultants). It is difficult to say that this practice should not be allowed. The arguments for allowing the auditor to render management services is that he is an expert in the field and that he knows the firm or organization because in the course of his search for evidence he became familiar with it. By engaging him to render additional services, the client saves the costs of acquiring information that is necessary in order to render the services. The auditor already knows the operations, while another consultant would have to acquire first the knowledge of the actual situation.

The increased efficiency constitutes an advantage for the society as a whole. It seems that we have to live with the situation, but we do not have to live with it and hide it. The first step toward the solution could be the disclosure in the "auditor's report" of the fact that the auditor is not completely detached from management but that in certain areas he is part of the management since management has asked for his advice. The form of the auditor's report should not be identical in the two situations. It should be worded differently in cases when the auditor acted independently from the directors and management and in cases when he was, in effect, part of the management team and was an advisor to the directors and the management. The two types of audit reports would clear the meaning of the opinion and would acknowledge the lack of independence when it was not needed.

If we look around, we find that the auditor's independence is not a requirement in closely held corporations, private companies, and partnerships. The recognition of the auditor's liability when he is part of the management team, in situations where in reality he is not independent, would improve the situation and would disperse the uncertainty existing in the minds of the persons who may rely on his opinion.

The problem of independence and the application of the principle of independence of judgment is more complex in the area of operational and internal audit. In organizations that make use of the operational and internal audit functions, the auditors do not usually perform the ultimate audits that result in an opinion or judgment. Their work is confined to search for evidence about past and present operations. The evidence, which is usually the function of direct communications, by-passes the daily organizational bottlenecks and filters. With their activity they provide information that is otherwise withheld, blocked, or unseen by lower management. The final stage of the audit function—the opinion, judgment, or decision to be made—is usually exercised by top management, based on evidence provided by the internal or operational auditor. The operational or internal auditor has to establish the evidence, and this is also an audit function and activity. We can compare his work to the procedures that the trial judge follows in establishing and verifying evidence. The auditor's purpose is to answer the question, What is the reality, the actual situation? He applies the norms: (1) Is it real? (2) Is it the best? (3) Are the proper procedures being followed? Next he searches for evidence. His report is a judgment, an opinion, to the responsible level of management. In possession of the report, which is the result of a historical (past) or contemporary (present) audit, the directors or top-level officials of the organization have to make the judgment: Is corrective action necessary? And if the answer is yes, of what nature? Their action is of a decision-making character. Therefore, the independence requirement for the internal auditor is different from that for the shareholders auditor. It is enough if he can be sure that he will not gain advantages or suffer setbacks originated by the personnel in the audited areas as a consequence of his report to the higher level of management. On paper it is easy to fulfill this requirement; in practice it may be very difficult because the power structure of an organization is never constant.

COMPLETENESS OF THE JUDGMENT

The principle of completeness of judgment, opinion, or decision states that the judgment, opinion, or decision has to be conclusive. It cannot be qualified to the extent of invalidation. The judgment has to serve its purpose. In the absence of a definite opinion, further action may be required by the user (the decision maker) before he converts his decision into action. The relationship of the judgment to the purpose is just one aspect of the "completeness." Other aspects relate to the norms and the evidence and to their relationship to the judgment.

A good or complete judgment requires that in the process of making the judgment, the norms to be used shall be applied consistently and to their full extent. There shall not be a shifting of norms in order to create a desired judgment. We discussed this requirement under the heading of the principle of objectivity of norms. The principle of completeness of the judgment is closely related to the above-mentioned principle of objectivity of norms, but instead of pointing at the norms to be applied, it points at the process of application of the norms. The norms have to be applied to their full extent.

The same is true of the evidence created in the imagination

of the judge or maker of an opinion. If the norms and evidence are on hand and if the purpose requires a judgment, the full set of norms will be compared to the complete model of evidence, and a judgment or opinion should be arrived at.

We could explain the meaning of the principle by looking at a few examples: The classical example for a historical or past audit is that performed by the judge in the criminal court. A person is accused by the prosecutor of committing a murder. The evidence established by the court finds no murder victim, but it indicates that the accused committed a theft. The principle of completeness requires that the judge or opinion maker shall apply the full set of norms: The evidence does not correspond to the definition of premeditated murder; therefore, the accused is found not guilty in the murder case. If the procedural rules allow it, the judge has to apply the full set of norms—other provisions of the Criminal Code—and find the accused guilty of theft.

Procedural rules may very well prevent the judge from making a "complete" judgment, as for practical reasons the "completeness" of judgment is restricted: his freedom of judgment is formally limited by the accusation. Therefore, a criminal court's decision is not necessarily complete. To avoid the necessity of repeating the court proceedings, the prosecutors usually include in the accusations a whole array of acts falling under different provisions of the Criminal Code to allow the judge to make a "complete judgment."

Completeness of judgment in relationship to the evidence means that the "whole" evidence, or the "complete" evidence, shall be taken into consideration in the process of making a judgment. Naturally, the total evidence is infinite; it has no limit. We have to satisfy ourselves with a more or less restricted section of the past or future as evidence in constructing our mental model used in making the judgment. The available evidence has to be enough to allow a judgment to be made. If there is enough material and a judgment is still not made, the principle of completeness is violated but in a negative sense. If, on the other hand, material evidence is disregarded without proper reason, the judgment is incomplete in a positive sense.

A typical example of the violation of the principle of completeness in the negative sense is the judgment or opinion that consists of the listings of advantages and disadvantages of a decision without coming to a conclusion. We all know persons who are full of wisdom and information and who are always ready to discuss the expected results of a decision but who never make a decision. They are violating the principle of completeness in the negative sense. All the necessary components are present for a judgment and the situation requires it, but the judgment is not presented. The positively incomplete (and therefore false) judgment, opinion, or decision is more common. Gossip, guesses, and acceptance of hearsay or slanted evidence are the best examples. Gossiping men or women rarely exercise the necessary critical procedures; they accept hearsay evidence as facts. They make judgments without knowing what criteria they apply or do not apply.

But we have to add a word of caution. We may arrive at a more or less complete judgment in the case of a historical (past) or present audit. Norms, evidence, and the like, may be established. The situation is different in the case of an anticipatory (future) audit, which is necessary in order to arrive at a judgment or decision on something in the future. Opinions about future happenings are always based on assumptions or projections. The most elementary is the assumption of time, that the future will become the present. Time is an abstraction based on the sequence of our memories. We extrapolate this experience in the future; we expect "things to happen." We also have to assume that the world surrounding us with the existing or slightly changing institutions, people, and so forth, will continue to exist. Therefore, the anticipatory judgment, decision, or opinion is incomplete. We may say that the more the underlying assumptions and the more the possibility for changes in the future, the less complete is our anticipatory judgment or opinion.

We may conclude by stating that no anticipatory judgment or decision is absolutely complete. The completeness of a decision can be evaluated, or audited, as the anticipated events happen or are supposed to happen. The model of expected future evidence can be compared to actual evidence, and the decision can be audited. Its completeness, in retrospect, has to be evaluated and corrected;

new decisions have to be made. The possibility and need for future evaluation and judgment on past decisions lead us to some important practical rules:

1. The longer the anticipated time span in the norms to be applied or in the anticipated model of evidence, the less complete the judgment on the future. The less complete the judgment underlying a decision, the greater the probability that the decision is incorrect.

In the literature and textbooks on capital investment decisions, we find mathematical models for selecting among alternatives in making investment decisions. The essence of one of them consists of the computation of the present value of the expected cash flow generated by the investment through its expected duration. Interest discount rates are assumed; the life of the object of the investment is assumed. The present value of the future benefits is then compared to the outlay necessary to produce it.

Another method is to determine the time span in which the investment will return in cash the outlay that is needed. It is evident that the second method produces better decisions because the judgment based on it is more complete. We are dealing with shorter time periods, and we can eliminate the use of assumed discount rates.

2. Decisions based on anticipatory (future) judgments or opinions have to be audited (reexamined) as the anticipated evidence (expected assumptions about the future) becomes present and past. The actual happenings or circumstances may invalidate the judgment underlying the decision. Therefore, decisions and actions that are based on anticipatory and more or less incomplete judgments or opinions have to be adjustable in order to reduce the damages from the incorrect judgments. It is commonplace to say that plans for future operations or budgets have to be adjusted in the light of actual evidence. In daily life and practice, we find this eternal problem: Accepted and approved plans for the future become masters instead of remaining servants; they have a hypnotic effect on individuals and groups. Master plans or budgets develop into goals as they are organized into normative schemata in the memory of the individuals who would be supposed to audit or reevaluate the decisions in the light of the actual evidence

as it developed variances from the anticipated one.

The history of the Second World War supplies ample examples of this phenomenon. After the facts become known, Hitler was considered to have been a madman for not having adjusted his plans that seemed reasonable to him and his advisors in 1939 and 1940. There is still a polite silence about Roosevelt and his advisors, who, because they were unable or unwilling to change their preconceived ideas, failed to adjust their line of action in the light of ample evidence in 1944 about the intentions of Stalin.

COMMUNICABILITY OF THE JUDGMENT

The principle of communicability of the judgment or opinion applies to opinions to be used by others and not by the judge alone. It states that the judgment has to be expressed in a form and a language that are understood, not misunderstood, by the potential user.

The judgment of another represents data for the potential user. Those data may be used or rejected by persons perceiving them. They will go through the screening process of information processing, and they will be stored in the memory, attached to certain schemata, and eventually used for making further judgments, for decisions.

We have to differentiate between opinions that appear only once (for example, verbal statements made within a certain context at a given time and directed toward a known user or users) and opinions that are laid down in some permanent form, written down and usable by anybody in the future. Accordingly, we have to consider three basic situations:

1. The opinion (message) is directed to a receiver who is programmed or prepared to receive it. The receiver may have formulated and defined the purpose of the audit, and the answer may be given in the required form, length, and so forth. The judge in this case has to see that the opinion will be given in the required form and at a time when disturbing concurrent data will not prevent or distort its reception and understanding (the data-information process).

2. The opinion is directed to a potential user who is not preprogrammed to receive the data. This is the case when an

opinion or judgment is communicated to a person or a group who is using it for a purpose that was not anticipated by the auditor or judge. The opinion has to be rendered under conditions that caution the receiver against processing it incorrectly. It has to be in a form that is understandable by the receiver, in plain terms and, if necessary, with explanations and with the reasoning included to support the opinion.

The auditor or judge has to make sure that the opinion is not misunderstood by the receiver and, if possible, he must test the understanding, the resulting information, on the part of the receiver.

The best method of testing the information created by the receiver is by requesting feedback, if this is possible. The feedback may develop into an exchange of supplementary data until both parties are satisfied that the opinion or judgment has been properly communicated and understood. If feedback is not possible, the opinion has to be expanded and stated in terms that render it difficult for the receiver to misunderstand or create "not intended" information.

The auditor has to know the words, concepts, and ideas that are familiar to the receiver; and he has to construct his opinion using the words known, taking into consideration the connotations, concepts, and ideas evoked by his verbal or written statement. The longer the opinion, the lower the intensity of the message; but short opinions or messages lack the power of persuasion.[7] In human society, short judgments or opinions seem to be the results of a short and, therefore, superficial process of judgment. We often hear people repeating an opinion several times. By repeating it they do not convey new data, and the receiver will not gain new information. They just show that they attach importance to the opinion made and they want to indicate the firmness of their stand in order to back up the opinion.

3. The auditor or judge is more or less in control of the information created by the potential user in cases 1 and 2. The problem of communicability is more complex if the opinion or

---

[7] Lawrence Revsine, "Data Expansion and Conceptual Structure," *Accounting Review* (October, 1970), pp. 701–11.

judgment is laid down in writing and anybody can use it to make decisions, relying on the opinion without the knowledge of the auditor or judge.

The laid-down written opinion is a potential source of data for anybody who may read it. The information created by the user of the data is beyond the control of the person creating the opinion. How can we ensure that the data will not be misinterpreted or misused? One remedy is to lay down the purpose of the opinion, the evidence available and accepted (a subjudgment), the norms applied, the limitations of effort and time imposed on the procedures and the judgment, and the prevailing circumstances at the time of the judgment. An example of this type of opinion is the unabbreviated final judgment of the trial court in criminal or civil cases.

A written opinion that fulfills the above-mentioned requirements would be so lengthy that very few could afford the energy and time to produce it, and even fewer could afford the energy and time to read it and eventually use it. The limitations of everyday life render this impossible, except in special cases.

The effort required to receive data is in an inverse relationship to the probability of the reception and to the probability of the data becoming an information. The shorter and stronger the message (the data), the stronger the probability of its being used by the receiver. But if the message is too short, it can be missed completely. Short data have to be repeated in order to ensure reception.

For practical purposes the solution lies between the two extremes. Every person who expresses an opinion or judgment in a form that is usable subsequently by others has the duty of safeguarding subsequent and distant users from using the opinion when it is no longer usable or from using it out of context.

There are no absolute safeguards against misinterpretation of data without the opportunity to control the resulting information (feedback). But the author of the opinion has to try everything he can in order to prevent the misuse of the data. The message has to be short enough but not too short; detailed enough but not too detailed; plain and simple enough but not so general that it loses its usefulness. If the auditor (the author of the opinion) is aware of potential or actual misuses or misinterpretations of the opinion, his duty is to warn against these dangers and, if possible, to take corrective actions.

THE PRINCIPLES OF EVIDENCE

The most dangerous and difficult area in every judgment (or audit) is that of the evidence. Except for very easy everyday actions, when we are in immediate contact with the evidence (as in a "concurrent" audit), we have to rely on groups of surrogates and interim opinions communicated to us verbally or in writing.

We may develop the following five principles dealing primarily with the area of evidence:

1. The principle of availability.
2. The principle of independence in gathering evidence.
3. The principle of directness.
4. The principle of confirmation.
5. The principle of bias.

AVAILABILITY OF EVIDENCE

Stating the principle of availability of evidence almost sounds like stating a triviality. No judgment or evaluation is possible without sufficient evidence. We may nod approvingly, and we may decide to skip over the next page of discussion. But stop for a moment! How many judgments do we make without having adequate evidence, by simply imitating statements taken over from strangers, friends, newspapers, or books?

Often-repeated statements, judgments, and opinions become stereotyped truths, confirmed by social pressures. I remember watching on TV an honorable member of the United States Senate, who was talking about the next day's "sensation," some witnesses in the case of the investigation of the alleged "crimes" of a very senior United States administrator. The speaker introduced the witnesses who were to be on the screen the next day. The TV reporter asked him the question, "Do you think he is guilty?" "Of course, he is guilty," sounded the well-informed answer of the senator. "We are just searching for evidence to prove it."

After this nonsense I ceased attaching any credibility to the pronouncements of that committee of ignorant people.

Unfortunately we do not have access to the evidence used for all the statements, judgments, and forecasts that others are making, and in our everyday life we have to rely on many of them because we have to make decisions. We cannot live without relying on others as sources of data (surrogates). We are very rarely in a position to make an "investigation of attitudes" in order to arrive at an opinion about the reliability of the assertion that we have to deal with. In our daily living, we grope around half-blind, led by others who are half- or totally blind informants.

It is a big step in the right direction if we are aware of the situation and realize the inherent weakness of our position.

In audits, investigations, judgments, and decisions involving material interest, we have to abstain from statements, opinions, and so forth, unless we are in possession of satisfactory evidence. We may negate the statement or qualify it, describing the limits of available evidence, or simply state, "I cannot come to a conclusion."

But what happens if a decision is required without data or information being available? In this case, we have to take the risk and responsibility, and we have to be ready to face the impending consequences.

INDEPENDENCE IN GATHERING EVIDENCE ("OPERATIONAL INDEPENDENCE"[8])

We have mentioned and discussed the meaning of "independence" earlier. But we have to bring it up again as it applies to the area of evidence.

The auditor has the task of arriving at an interim judgment on the extent of the evidence presented or available. The evidence may be too narrow; some clues that make the reconciliation of surrogates difficult have to be cleared up; additional investigation may be necessary. If we are not in a position to extend the scope of evidence and follow up the clues, our final opinion or judgment will suffer. The extension of the limits of the surrogates available, the investigation of clues, takes energy and time.

---

[8] H. A. Sharaf and R. K. Mautz, "An Operational Concept of Independence," *Journal of Accountancy* (April, 1960).

Restrictions imposed on the auditor in this endeavor have a
negative effect on the quality of the evidence available to him.
The restrictions may be imposed by circumstances that are beyond
the control of the auditor (e.g., by statutes or by limitations set
by the nature of the assignment) or by limitations of available
time and energy that are imposed by the auditor himself (e.g.,
by deadlines). If I have to accept every surrogate at "face value"
and if I do not want to search for clues, I will only fill out the
usual working papers and meet all my deadlines. I will not perform
an audit. I will attach only tick marks to certain documents and
will do a good clerical job. The operational type of independence
is extremely important in group audits. The person who signs
the final opinion, the one who renders the judgment, relies on
information provided by the persons or groups working "in the
field." We cannot see the clues that they could discover by
comparing surrogates at a lower level of generalization. But we
can come up with a general recommendation: Inform the field
staff properly about purpose, norms (criteria), risks, and so forth,
and train them properly.

The field staff has to be expert in the realities, the practices
prevailing in the circumstances; it has to know the theoretical
backbone of the evaluation and judgment process. It also has
to be aware of the dangers and risks that it may cause. The study
of big blunders by judges or auditors in recent liability cases is
the best study material for developing a feel for standards in
the procedures related to the evaluation of the evidence.

Perhaps the best instrument of evaluation for young auditors
is the case history of liability suits against auditors and the history
of frauds. The cheapest way of acquiring experience is to get
vicarious experience by learning about errors committed by others.
With proper theoretical foundation, the vicarious experience is
more fruitful and efficient than apprenticeship without education
in fundamentals (the theory of auditing). An apprentice may learn
about the environment in which he works; he may learn to imitate
the standard procedures; but without knowing the reasons for
the work he does, he will not be in a position to evaluate or
judge nor will he be able to see the importance of the clues that
he is missing.

DIRECTNESS OF EVIDENCE

The principle of directness (distance, reliability) of evidence concentrates on the quality of surrogates that are available for the auditor or judge. The event (principal) is represented by surrogates to the person who is attempting to arrive at an opinion on the event. The surrogates may be closer to the event (e.g., the description of an eyewitness) or less close (e.g., the description of a person who met an eyewitness and listened to his story). In this respect the principle is the expression of the empirical fact that the communication of data changes the originally perceived and represented principal with every step of communications.

Distance has a second meaning. It is in the field of the data pyramid. In this second sense it means the conceptual extent (level of generality) of the surrogates. Surrogates are at different levels of generalization.

The structure of criteria (norm system) requires that the surrogates of evidence shall be at the same level of generalization as the categories (pigeonholes) in the norm system (criteria). Without this requirement, a proper synopsis, resulting in a correct opinion or judgment, is impossible.

If I have to express an opinion on the statements listing different assets and liabilities, I have to express the surrogates at the same level of generalization as that required by my system of criteria (norm system).

I may have an item: "Building—cost $100,000." If the building was purchased recently and no other building is owned by the makers of the statement, I will have to look for a surrogate of the original transaction (principal). I may find a sales contract indicating a purchase price of $99,000 and legal costs of $1,000. The two surrogates are at a lower level of generalization; my concept of cost includes both the consideration and the legal costs. The two available surrogates are at the next level of generalization; and since the "distance" is small, the probability of arriving at a correct judgment is high.

Now, let us assume that the building was not purchased but was constructed by the client, who is in the construction business.

The surrogates at the transaction level are numerous payments for direct labor, payments for raw materials, payments and charges for overhead (including indirect labor, depreciation of equipment, etc.). Some of those payments are identified with the activity necessary to erect the building and are grouped (added) together in order to arrive at the total figure of the cost of the building. A series of interim surrogates (representations of management) are available at higher levels of generalization; they are based on cost allocations, measurements, inferences, and judgments. The distance between the surrogates at the transactions level (primary surrogates) and the final $100,000 cost is considerable. With the distance, the possibility and probability of errors increase. If the possibility of errors increases, the reliability (or correctness) of the evidence is of a lower quality.

CONFIRMATION OF EVIDENCE

The principle of confirmation ("stereo" communication) of evidence applies to the reliability (truth value) of the surrogates. It states that the surrogates from a single source are less reliable than surrogates that originate from different sources and confirm each other. A surrogate may go through a chain of underlying surrogates, a chain of communication processes. Each communication process is a potential source of errors. (Data may be incorrectly organized and received and erroneously interpreted, and wrong inferences may be drawn.) The chances are that two independent chains of communication will reveal the errors by resulting in surrogates with differences. By reconciling the surrogates the auditor can confirm them, or he can detect irreconcilable differences (clues) that have to be clarified by further investigation.

It is interesting to note that in England and North America the standards set by the courts and professional bodies gradually required the confirmation of more and more component items in the financial statements audited by the shareholders auditor.

Prior to the First World War, the confirmation principle was applied to the Cash and Marketable Securities. In the twenties of our century, the Receivables had to be confirmed, too, by sending out confirmation requests to creditors. In the thirties, the confirmation of the Inventories was recommended not only by asking for a meaningless letter from management but also by requiring that the auditor or his agent be present at and review the stock-taking procedures. The next step was the confirmation of the Liabilities and the physical inspection of Fixed Asset items. We may say that in the seventies all items of the financial statements have to be confirmed, at least by sampling the numerous small balances that compose the balances under one heading.

According to modern standards the reliance on internally derived surrogates alone is not enough. The auditor has to confirm those surrogates by developing surrogates from external sources which are not controlled or controllable by the actions of the auditees.

One of many famous mistrials took place in South Africa around 1900. A murder was committed, and a man was accused of the murder. There was only one witness who allegedly had seen the murder. The witness described the murder in every detail. The nature of the injuries and other circumstances (time, location, clothing of the victim, etc.) corroborated the testimony of the witness. The accused denied having any knowledge of the murder, but he could not satisfy the court that he was somewhere else during the time of the crime. The accused was found guilty on the testimony of the witness and was executed. Later, just before his death, the former witness confessed that he had committed perjury and that it was not the accused but he himself who had committed the murder.

In the case, the court accepted a group of surrogates originating from one source, the real murderer. The other surrogate, a sheer denial, was rejected. The principle of confirmation was not applied.

Following that case and other possible similar cases, provisions were made in the relevant statutes of every civilized country to prevent the miscarriage of justice by the nonapplication of the principle of confirmation. (The Criminal Code of Canada, Statute 684: "No person accused of an offence under any one of the hereunder mentioned sections shall be convicted upon the evidence of one witness unless such witness is corroborated in some material particular by evidence implicating the accused. . . .")

The high risks involved in convicting persons on insufficient or false evidence originating from one source without confirmation justify the provisions of the statutes. We have to note that the principle of confirmation is inherent also to double-entry book-keeping. Debits and credits have to balance.

BIAS OF EVIDENCE

Our discussion of the principle of confirmation leads us to the principle of bias (risk) in the interpretation of surrogates and in the extent of confirmation required. This principle states that in the evaluation of surrogates and in the evaluation of the array of surrogates required, we shall take into consideration the potential damages and risks that we could suffer or could cause others to suffer.

On the surface the principle of bias seems to contradict the principle of objectivity through "freedom from bias." In reality, it is a necessary corollary of it. Freedom from bias (emotional objectivity) is not a justification for hasty judgments on questionable evidence (surrogates).

Our daily life presents ample restrictions and very often requires immediate decisions (yes or no) on surrogates that are not confirmable because of restrictions of time, expertise, lack of power, and so forth. If we are at least aware of the potential damages and risks that we have to take, we will come up with better opinions and judgments.

The principle of bias has two aspects. The first one applies to the acceptability of surrogates (as truth) and their interpretation (inferences made). In high-risk audits or judgments, we have to explore more clues, and we have to question the inferences made from the surrogates. Also, we have to expand the array of surrogates available, and this is the second aspect of the principle.

In the previously mentioned South African case, the principle of bias was not applied. The court accepted as true surrogates the ones presented by the witness (the actual murderer) and rejected the ones (sheer denial) presented by the accused.

What was the danger of the error? On one side, an innocent person was murdered by a false witness who used the court as an instrument in committing a murder by his perjury; on the other side, an unsolved case of murder remained.

The higher risk involves an extension (confirmation) of the surrogates and an exploration (investigation) of all possible inferences made from the already available surrogates. Nobody explored the possible inference from the testimony of the witness: If he knew all the details, he might be not only a witness but also the murderer.

We hear the legal term "beyond reasonable doubt" as a requirement in establishing an evidence from the available surrogates. Unfortunately, the meaning of "reasonable doubt" is different for different people. Emotional style, pressures of time, and other such considerations endanger the consistent application of the guideline. On the other hand, we may carry reasonable doubt too far. We may have reasonable doubt even in our own perceptions and arrive at a stage when we refrain from all opinion, decision, and action.

CONCLUSION

The expression *standards of auditing* has two meanings. It can be interpreted as the total of the rules, guidelines laid down by an authoritive body to be followed in the performance of an audit; or it can describe the actual quality of performance in case of an individual audit.

For the public accounting profession the standards are laid down in statutes and pronouncements of the AICPA and SEC in the U.S. For an internal auditor the standards could be laid down in instructions from management or in formal programs. An operational auditor or management consultant may adhere to his own personal standards, depending on his experience.

The standards can be good, conducive to performing a good audit, if they allow the auditor to follow the principles of auditing. They may be poor if they violate the principles outlined earlier in Chapters VII and VIII. The standards connect the theory with the practice. Without theory we are unable to have an opinion about the standards. Without theory we are unable to improve them.

It is beyond the scope of the present work to describe the standards from organized sources or from practical experience. The established textbooks in auditing already do a good job in describing them. But standards are continuously changing as the authorities try to satisfy the expectations of users and regulation bodies. These changes try to promote the quality and efficiency of the audit function. In order to achieve this goal, they have to be supported by an exhaustive and philosophically sound theory of auditing. The aim of this book has been to provide the foundations and the theory.

INDEX